EFFECT OF
MOTIVATION AND COPING WITH STRESS

Ms.CHANDANA SHET

TABLE OF CONTENTS

LIST OF TABLES

Table

Page

LIST OF FIGURES

CHAPTER- I

INTRODUCTION

Introduction

Parents provide children with the framework from which they can begin to develop and cultivate their own value system. This framework is developed by socialization, observation and interactions that children have with their parents. Modelling is a powerful, indirect tool through which children learn the most without parents realizing what they are teaching their children. Hence, it is very important for parents to be conscious of their behaviour as they will unknowingly be imitated by their children. The process of the transmission of the values and habits from parents to children begins at a young age and can have lasting effects on the future of individuals, as well as socialization for generations to come. Darling and Steinberg (1993) defined parenting as practices which are visible, specific behaviours that are directed towards socializing with their children. According to Curtis and Newman (2004), parenting is a family dynamic that often has a direct impact on and within a family. Hence, parenting is an important and necessary area to be researched upon. There are studies of Baumrind (1997); Muller and Kerbow (1993) on parenting which illustrate and examine its impact on children in different ways. Appropriate parenting becomes very vital at the stage of adolescence because this is a crucial stage for identity formation.

The word 'adolescence' has a Latin origin, and means to grow or to mature. It is a period of transition where an individual evolves, both physically and psychologically from a child to an adult. The period of adolescence has been described as the period of awakening and self-discovery with regard to physical, social, intellectual and emotional competencies. The individual's physical, mental, social, moral and spiritual attitudes go through revolutionary changes. Such changes, during adolescence, are more rapid than during infancy or childhood. During adolescence, the individual wants to make independent decisions in various situations, which may be regarded as an act of indiscipline by the adults around. However, gradually the adolescent starts to regulate one's desires according to the standards set by the society, and begins to realize the social responsibilities.

Adolescence was described by Piaget as that life stage in which egocentric thoughts reduce and more abstract thinking begins. This allows the individual to think and reason with a wider perspective. Their changing mind, body, and relationships are often the cause of stress, as this change, they assume is something to be feared (Campbell & Ntobedzi, 2007).

Adolescence is a time of life when the child is on the threshold of adulthood. It is a period of intense and rapid development and is characterized by numerous developmental tasks including gaining new and more mature relationship with others, achieving emotional independence from parents and the cognitive and psychological resources to face the challenges of adult life (Hazen, Schlozman & Beresin, 2008). Thus, this is the time when the responsibilities of a mature adult are slowly becoming manifested in the child's mind. The adolescent mind is filled with dreams for the future, and perhaps even some fantasy. Adolescents acquire the increasing ability to think abstractly and hypothetically. They can picture situations that did not occur (Steinberg & Silk, 2002). In Adolescence, children have to undergo many difficulties and have to deal with problems of being under the scrutiny of adults which many do not like. Coping resources during adolescence include those aspects of the self, like, problem-solving skills, interpersonal skills, and the social environment aspect like availability of supportive social network that facilitate successful adaptation to life stressors. In developmental and family psychology, the widely researched topics have been parenting styles and its influence on parent-child bond. Previous research has shown that parenting styles are one of the most imperative factors among other family factors that influence parent-adolescent relationships (Shek, 2002). Therefore, parenting becomes even more significant at the stage of adolescence as it is the stepping stone towards adulthood.

There are various factors which are important for a healthy and effective development of the child like effective study habits, motivation and coping with any kind of stress. These factors affect a student academically, emotionally and socially. Study habits are learner's habitual ways of exercising and practicing their abilities for learning (Yazdani & Godbole, 2014). Motivation is generally defined as internal condition that stimulates, directs and maintains behaviour (Woolfolk, 2004). Coping with stress is the cognitive and behavioural efforts an individual uses to manage specific demands or stressors (Folkman & Lazarus, 1980).

There are different behavioural, emotional and social issues that students face. Amongst the overall issues, maximum cases are related to anxiety, inattention, lack of motivation, poor academic performance etc. Further research attributes this to faulty study habits, poor motivation and non-influencing/ supportive home learning environment. Additionally, these problems are worsened at the stage of adolescence, with lack of problem solving skills and low frustration tolerance. Poor problem solving, decision making skills and low tolerance for frustration can make students resort to inappropriate ways of handling stress which ultimately point to poor coping skills. There are research models that highlight central role of parents in developing and /or maintaining childhood disorders (Clarke, Cooper, & Creswell, 2013) as children's emotional well-being is majorly shaped by parents and this effect is highest during the early years of childhood (Gar, Hudson, & Rapee, 2005). Hence, it is understood that children's coping skills are affected by their parents coping skills. Thergaonkar and Wadkar (2007), said that despite there not being one parenting theory which is complete and conclusive, there is still evidence that parenting style is the most influential factor for child development. Researchers are interested to understand the prominence of parenting practices in influencing child development, and how family experiences act together to impact childrens' behavioural and developmental outcomes (Collins, Maccoby, Steinberg, Hetherington, & Bornstein, 2000). A home and family is a place where child's basic needs of food and safety get fulfilled. This is also a place where major psychological needs of belongingness, emotional security and self-esteem get satisfied. Thus, the family provides a basis for children to shape their personalities and improve their potential abilities to the optimum level. The adolescent's achievements and success in life depends on the social learning and the parenting style one has received in the family. According to Kumar (2014), parenting style along with other social influence may be held responsible for children's self-esteem, self-confidence, friendly disposition, self-reliance, curiosity, ability to cope with stress, resilience and achievement orientation.

Therefore, the child comes to school not as an independent individual but as a part of a family environment and this environment influences the emotional development and personality of the child. Researchers have always been interested in the importance of parenting and the consequent impact it has on the behaviour and development of the child. (Collins, Maccoby, Steinberg, Hetherington, & Bornstein, 2000). The aim of this research is to study in detail about study habits, achievement motivation, coping skills and parenting. Parenting can be broadly defined as the general behaviours and attitudes of a caregiver in interactions with their child (Morris, Silk, Steinberg, Myers & Robinson, 2007). Parental attitudes and behaviours that are performed while raising children have a significant impact on children's future behaviour as well as shaping behaviour at early ages. Children must have healthy relationships with their parents in order to display consistent behaviours in society, to be self-sufficient, to gain necessary social skills, and achieve his/her independence. This is closely related with parental attitudes and behaviours; i.e. the parenting styles that the parents adopt (Akca, 2012).

Brooks (1991) has shared a simple definition of parenting wherein he mentions that it is being in the state of a parent and providing the child with nourishment, protection and guidance. Parenting style refers to a combination of parental behaviours which are consistently used across different settings and are characterized by levels of warmth, responsiveness, control, and punishment. Although many conceptualizations of parenting styles have been delineated, most of the studies are dedicated to the amount and quality of responsiveness/warmth, control/demandingness, and discipline in the parent (Power, 2013). Nancy and Laurance (1993) described the parenting styles as "a constellation of attitudes toward the child that are communicated to the child and that, taken together, create an emotional climate in which the parent's behaviours are expressed". Most researchers have accepted the categorization of the parenting style given by Baumrind (1971), which is mainly based on the interaction between parent and child along two dimensions: parental control/demandingness and parental warmth/ responsiveness. This resulted in three types of parenting style, namely permissive, authoritative, and authoritarian parenting styles.

A permissive parent has less demands from the child and grants high levels of autonomy. An authoritative parent is receptive to the child, has high demands, and grants necessary autonomy. An authoritarian parent is less responsive to the child, has high demands which may not match child's potential, and grants little autonomy. Permissive parenting style was additionally differentiated into permissive-indulgent and permissive-indifferent parenting style by Maccoby and Martin (1983). While permissive-indulgent parents (referred to as permissive parents) are greatly involved in children's lives and are highly responsive, permissive-indifferent parents (referred to as uninvolved or neglectful parents) are detached, and exhibit low levels of both responsiveness and demandingness. The detailed description of these styles are as follows:

Authoritarian-Parenting

Authoritarian style tends to be high on demandingness and low in responsiveness (Huver, Otten, Vries & Engels, 2009). Compliance, conformity, parental control and respect for authority are the major concern of authoritarian parents. They prefer exercising high degree of demands on their children rather than nurturance and open communication. Children from authoritarian homes will be punished when they disobey the strict rules and regulations which are set by their parents. Authoritarian parents usually discourage autonomy and disallow decision making by their children (Bornstein & Zlotnik, 2008). Authoritarian parents restrain children's self-expression and freedom desires, and use power-assertive techniques (physical force, love withdrawal, commands, threats) to achieve what they want from their children (Zupancic et al., 2004). They focus on success aspects and love is conditional with achievement. They are less nurturing than the other two styles of parenting (Berg, 2011). These parents want their orders to be followed by their children without any excuse. Children from these families tend to be dependent and/or rebellious. Rebellious adolescents exhibit aggressive behaviours, whereas obedient/submissive adolescents can be dependent on their families (Baumrind, 1991).

Authoritative-Parenting

Baumrind (1991) stated that authoritative parenting style is high in both demandingness and responsiveness (Pellerin, 2005). Authoritative parents apply firm control and require their children obey with a reasonable set of rules and guidelines. They utilize reason and control to make disciplinary decisions while harsh forms of punishment are discouraged to use (Bornstein & Zlotnik, 2008). Authoritative parenting style provides warmth, love, and acceptance for their children in order to educate them to become progressively more autonomous. Another important characteristic that needs to be highlighted is verbal give-and-take between parents and children. Open communication and reciprocal dialogue can be found within this parenting style (Dwairy & Menshar, 2005). These parents monitor and regulate children's attitude, while at the same time, provide support and warmth (Baumrind, 1971). They pay attention to children's compliance and set standard rules while providing autonomy to children. They acknowledge their kids' perspective, provide them freedom in choice making and empower their children's' opinion in family matters (Berg, 2011; Zupancic, Podlesek, & Kavcic, 2004). This type of family atmosphere provides young individuals with occasions to trust themselves within certain limits and to develop a healthy autonomy. Children raised in this type of family structure develop as individuals who have self-confidence, entrepreneurship, creativity, are able to express their thoughts and produce alternative solutions to problems (Kopko, 2007).

Permissive-Parenting

Baumrind stated that permissive (indulgent parenting style) is high on responsiveness and low on demandingness, and rarely enforce rules for their children to follow (Snell, Overbey, & Brewer, 2005). Permissive parents are different than authoritarian parents. They practice high level of nurturance and clarity of communication while exercising low level of control and demands (Bornstein & Zlotnik, 2008). Permissive parents encourage autonomy and decision making by their children. They tend to accept and support greatly towards impulses, needs, and behaviours of their children and avoid confrontation and punishment (Dwairy & Menshar, 2005). Permissive parents allow their children to experience a high level of freedom and do not impose rules and regulation to restrain their practices, unless physical harm is expected (Rossman & Rea, 2005). Permissive-indulgent parents are warm, cuddly and responsive, convey low level of parental control, they provide little direction and instruction to their children (Edwards, 1999). However, they show high level of parental support and emotional nurturance (Gullota, Blau, & Ramos, 2007). This type of parenting may cause difficulties for the adolescents in controlling themselves and may result in egocentric behaviours (Baumrind, 1991). The permissive and unstructured attitudes of the parents cause children to be spoilt and expect that they will be given priority over the other individuals in the society. When they are not given priority, the individuals feel restless and uncomfortable and cannot adjust to social relationships outside the family (Akca, 2012).

Further research by Maccoby and Martin also suggested the addition of a fourth parenting style – uninvolved/ neglectful parenting style (referred as indifferent parenting style) (Chan & Koo, 2010).

Uninvolved/ neglectful parenting style

Indifferent parents are neither responsive nor controlling to their children (Pellerin, 2005). They are not involved in parenting roles and are not interested in guiding for development of their children. Besides that, children coming from indifferent parenting style have less or no rules and regulations to obey. This parenting may create a lack of self-control in children. Moreover, children's self-respect and proficiency levels may be affected negatively (Baumrind, Larzelere & Owens, 2010).

Perceived parenting styles are defined as an opinion of adolescents or children about styles of parental behaviors during their childhood. According to the definition, assessment of children about parental behaviors is important. There are two types of perceived parenting styles: care and overprotection (Fonte, 2015). Student lives are said to be the best period for any person as the foundations for emotional intelligence, self-esteem, happiness, and success in life are laid in childhood and adolescence. This period is a phase of life where a person is in between childhood and adulthood. It is imperative that parents give enough support and guidance for them to deal with the stressors at different stages, which will give them a fruitful future.

McClelland investigated the possibility that differences in child-rearing practices in various societies and cultures accounted for differences in the development of motivation in individuals. He found that "child-rearing practices that emphasize independence training and mastery, produce people who are high in achievement motivation" (Maehr, Martin & Braskamp, 1986). According to Darling and Steinberg's (1993) integrative model, adolescents' behavioural outcomes are influenced by parenting styles and this happens in the way how adolescents accept their parents' efforts to socialize them. Adolescents do not remain passive beings, however are actively involved in molding the parent-child relationship and apply meaning to parenting behaviour and this ultimately affects their own outcome. Adolescents' lookout towards the given behavioural autonomy and the rightfulness of parental authority are important psychological processes (Darling, Cumsille & Martinez, 2007). Autonomy means the acts which are derived from oneself and not from others (Chen, Vansteenkiste, Beyers, Soenens & Petegem, 2013). Different parenting styles result in varied individual differences in adolescents' beliefs about autonomy. An adolescents' beliefs about autonomy can affect parent–adolescent relationship. Adolescents usually claim autonomy earlier than their parents are ready to grant it even though parents and adolescents expect increasing autonomy with age and this can result in conflicts (Jensen & Gozkan, 2015;

Perez, Cumsille & Martinez, 2016). Generally, adolescents' demand more autonomy than their parents are ready to give them and this, in turn, leads adolescents to apply more control over their issues, and consequently makes them criticize their parents controlling practices and this causes conflict and minimizes cohesion (Fuligni, 1998; Zhang & Fuligni, 2006). Along with developmental changes leading to autonomy, adolescence stage also brings in attitude change about parental authority, which then determines whether parental assertion of control will be seen as an adequate extension of their role (Darling, Cumsille & Martinez, 2008). Thus, parent–adolescent relationship are related to adolescents' outlook towards legitimacy of authority. Adolescents' acceptance of parental authority results in better cohesion and less conflicting encounters with parents (Zhang, Wang & Fuligni, 2006; Jensen & Gozkan, 2015). A study by Bi *et al.* (2018) examined the relation between parenting styles and parent-adolescent relationship factors. Results from a sample of 633 adolescents showed that there were similar levels of parent–adolescent conflict frequency for all parenting styles. However, the intensity of conflict was noted to be higher among youth of neglectful and authoritarian parents. The maximum level of cohesion with both mother and father were reported by adolescents with authoritative parents, followed by authoritarian, indulgent, and neglectful parenting styles. In context to youth with authoritative or indulgent mothers, cohesion was higher for girls than boys.

There is also a cultural difference which draws a thin line between parenting styles. Asian cultures adopt more authoritarian parenting as compared to the United States and Europe. Asian students exhibit more effective academic achievement with parents who have attributes of authoritarian parenting as compared to the West and European countries where the majority of students' academic achievement is the outcome of authoritative parenting. In one study Dornbusch, Ritter, Liederman, Roberts and Fraleigh (1987) found that parenting styles vary in different cultures. Authoritative parenting style affects European American adolescents for the better while authoritarian parenting improves the academic performance of Asian American adolescents. In another study, it was found that parents of Chinese American adolescents were stricter than European American parents which is a characteristic of authoritarian parenting style (Lin and Fu, 1990). To understand the cultural differences in China, Peterson, Steinmetz and Wilson (2005) conducted a detailed study and found two major factors. Firstly, China has been unique in the world because they had implemented one child policy until 2016. This significantly changed the family structure, which was then known as the "4-2-1" family structure (four grandparents, two parents, and one child). Therefore, the association of parenting styles with parent–adolescent conflict and cohesion in China may be different as compared to Western cultures. The Chinese culture emphasizes collectivist values such as following the social norms, compliance to authority, and avoiding confrontation. In this strict background, individuals' request for autonomy are not encouraged as that may potentially threaten group harmony, however unquestioning respect for parental authority is valued (Fuligni,

1998). Hence, autonomy and authority beliefs among adolescents differ according to cultural context. One study showed that intensity of conflict with mothers was higher when there was lower respect for parental authority in African American and Latina, but this was not observed among European American families (Dixon, Graber & Gunn, 2008). Another relevant, published study demonstrated that authoritative mothers exhibited the highest levels of cohesion with their children and authoritarian mothers displayed the lowest levels of cohesion (Zhang, Wei, Ji, Chen & Deckard, 2017).

Hence, it is understood that parenting styles and beliefs also get affected by social and cultural factors. Culture affects parenting, which is then maintained and transferred by parenting practices (Bornstein, 2012). Sorkhabi (2005) looked over many studies and found that Baumrind's (1971) typology is applicable across cultures. Parents in different cultures may recommend different parenting styles, but, all the three parenting styles can be seen in both collective and individualistic cultures.

Jacob and Seshadri (2013) mentioned that as objectives of socialization differ across cultures, parenting styles change as ideal developmental goals for parents differ according to the culture. Most important cultural difference between Western and Asian culture is the conception of independence versus interdependence (Wang & Leichtman, 2000). The independent/Individualistic cultures like USA and Europe emphasize on personal goals, whereas, interdependent/collectivistic societies like Asia, more importance is given to family and shared goals above the individual needs. Thus, Western cultures promote self-expression, independence, competitiveness, and self-sufficiency, while, obedience, conformity, respect for elders and social interdependence are expected by parents in Asian cultures (Keller & Otto, 2009). Due to varied cultural norms, children's developmental outcomes change depending on the cultural influence on parenting practices (Huang, Cheah, Lamb, & Zhou, 2017). Authoritarian parenting demands obedience and respect for authority. Since parents in Asia are more likely than Western parents to value interdependence, Asian parents hold more authoritarian attitudes, contributing to socialisation practices that lead to authoritarian parenting (Lansford et al., 2018). Accordingly, Asian adolescents may be more acceptable of parent control as parents generally use authoritarian styles and encourage subordination and co-dependent behaviour in their children (Mousavi, Low, & Hashim, 2016).

When the parent–child relationship is democratic, children are able to think independently, express their ideas, and behave freely. In a culture that values independence, parental control may conflict with adolescents need for independence and autonomy. Hence, parents in Western countries mostly use authoritative parenting styles which results in individualistic and independent behaviour in their children (Albert, Trommsdorff, & Mishra, 2007). The same parenting practice may not have the same effect across different cultures. In contrast, Br, Shroff & Raman (2019) found that the effect of parenting styles on children seem to be alike across culture, despite hypothesized cultural differences between the West and India. An authoritative parenting style was connected with better developmental outcome than authoritarian and neglectful/uninvolved parenting style in both Western countries and in India. However, findings on indulgent/ permissive parenting style were diverse in West as well as in India. Thus, there is need to consider different cultural contexts while interpreting parenting styles and parent-child relationships.

India is a country with diverse combination of languages, religions and ethnic groups and all of this has a unique influence on parenting. Conventionally, there is a joint family system wherein members live together and often assist in child rearing. However, currently there has been an ongoing social change with respect to family size, education, employment and role of women. In recent years, there has been a drop in nuclear families in urban areas and the same is on the rise in rural India (Registrar General of India, 2011). This may be because of pressures of long urban jobs, scarcity and expensive nature of housing, leading families to stay together. Additionally, there is an increasing number of working women (Registrar General of India, 2011). Consequently, both husband and wife being working, grandparents generally live with them to help take care of children. Along with the grandparents, older siblings too help care for their younger siblings in Indian families (Seema & Begum, 2008). This makes the Indian families diverse leading to different child-rearing practices. In India, breast-feeding is also a norm and maximum children are breastfed exclusively for the first six months, which is significantly high when compared to US where only 24.9% of children are exclusively breastfed through six months. Breast-feeding not only provides nourishment to the baby, but also allows increasing physical and emotional contact between mother and child. Traditions like cuddling and body massage add to physical contact between mother and child, and provides a sense of security for the child (Patel et al., 2015; Nimbalkar, Shukla, Phatak, & Nimbalkar, 2013)

In India, gender differences have been seen in parenting style. Normally, the father is considered as the head of the household and breadwinner of the family, whereas, mothers take on the responsibility of the house and childcare, like feeding, putting the child to bed or upholding discipline. Conventionally, fathers have been seen to have little involvement in childrearing, while, gender roles in India assume mothers to be nurturing caregivers (Barnhart, Raval, Jansari, & Raval, 2013). Hence, mothers, are viewed as more authoritative or permissive, but fathers are traditionally regarded as authoritarian (Barnhart, Raval, Jansari & Ravalet, 2013). However, active involvement of fathers in parenting is increasing leading to change in the traditional gender roles and resulting parenting styles (Bhattacharyya & Pradhan, 2015). Middle-class fathers in urban India are beginning to be actively involved in their children's lives because of more women engaging in workforce, and hence are becoming more nurturing, affectionate, and communicative in the daily lives of their children (Roopnarine, Talukder, Jain, Joshi, & Srivastav, 1990). Father's involvement reflects a cultural shift in the parenting styles and consequently in child outcomes as well.

Few researchers have tried to compare Indian parents with the parents in the West to pinpoint the differences in parenting styles. One study by Balda, Irving, Berthelsen, and Catherwood (2001) matched Indian parents to Australian parents, and noted that Indian parents were stricter and had more demands than Australian parents. Jambunathan and Counselman (2002) examined Indian mothers staying in the USA versus those residing in India, and observed that the mothers living in India favoured corporal punishment and were authoritarian. However, Indian mothers staying in USA adopted authoritative style of parenting. Similar findings were recounted in Canada, wherein, examiners found that European background adolescents in Canada mostly reported authoritative parenting, whereas Indian adolescents were more likely to state higher incidences of authoritarian parenting (Garg, Levin, Urajnik, & Kauppi, 2005). Another study by Albert, Trommsdorff and Mishraet (2007) matched Indian mothers with German mothers, and it was found that as compared to German mothers, Indian mothers described using more control and less acceptance. Overall, these studies show that Indian parents are more likely to use authoritarian parenting style making them highly demanding, less accepting, exerting more control and sometimes resorting to harsh punishment. But, these studies are more than a decade old, and hence cannot be applied to current times. Therefore, the current research will give us insight into parenting styles and its influence on important factors of study habits, achievement motivation and coping with stress.

Research by Masud, Ahmad and Thurasamy (2014) shows that all three parenting styles have effects on children's psychological, social, and moral development. Academic performance, problem solving behaviour, psychosocial development and social competence are among the vital domains which are affected by these parenting styles. Results from this research has shown that children who rate their parents as authoritative are socially and instrumentally more capable in academics as compared to those who perceive their parents as non-authoritative. Children who rate their parents as permissive perform poorly in all domains.

Among all the studies of western countries across ethnic groups and gender, authoritative parenting style seems to have the most positive child outcome when compared with other parenting styles. Authoritative parenting style was linked to children's wellbeing, adaptive behaviours and lesser child behaviour problems. It was found to be associated with greater subjective welfare, self-esteem, life-satisfaction, less depression and most optimum long term child development (King, Vidourek, & Merianos, 2016; Calafat, Garcia, Juan, Becona, & Fernandez-Hermida, 2014; Rinaldi & Howe, 2012; Luyckx et al., 2011; Milevsky, Schlechter, Klem, & Kehl, 2008; Milevsky, Schlechter, Netter & Keehn, 2007; Querido, Warner, & Eyberg, 2002). Students who had authoritative parents displayed better academic success. These students achieved higher GPAs, had better academic self-efficacy, used adaptive achievement strategies and problem coping, showed higher probabilities of continuing with education beyond school, and had fewer chances of having internalising and externalizing problems as adults (Steele & McKinney, 2018; Llorca, Cristina Richaud, & Malonda, 2017; Enten & Golan, 2009; Wolfradt, Hempel & Miles, 2003). Adolescents with authoritative parents had fewer chances of developing substance abuse than adolescents who perceived their parents as uninvolved (Calafat, Garcia, Juan, Becona & Hermida, 2014). These adolescents when compared with adolescents of other three parenting styles were less likely to engage in heavy drinking, had less chances of getting into smoking, cyber bullying or fighting, and also preferred to not have close friends using drugs or alcohol (Zurcher, Holmgren, Coyne, Barlett & Yang, 2018; Luyckx et al., 2011; Bahr & Hoffmann, 2010). Authoritative parenting (Zaborskis, Sirvyte, & Zemaitiene, 2016) along with parental warmth (Donath, Graessel, Baier, Bleich, & Hillemacher, 2014) were found to be protective factors against suicidal attempts among adolescents. Presence of one authoritative parent functioned as a shield from the harmful effects associated with less optimal parenting styles of the other parent. Having both parents as authoritative brought about most positive outcomes, with greater well-being connected with either both parents being authoritative or only authoritative mother as compared to no authoritative parent (Simons & Conger, 2007).

Calafat et al. (2014) shared that both permissive and authoritative parenting styles were found to have better outcomes than authoritarian and uninvolved parenting styles. Permissive parenting style was seen to have positive outcomes like active problem coping strategy (Wolfradt et al., 2003). Martinez, Fuentes, Garcia and Madrid (2013) reported that permissive parenting style can act as a protective factor for substance use, school misconduct and delinquent behaviour. Nevertheless, this does not signify that permissive parenting style results in good adjustment among children, as it has also been related to negative outcomes like antisocial behaviours (Luyckx et al., 2011). Williams et al. (2009) shared that problems of internalising were greatest among behaviourally withdrawn children whose parents were permissive. Low self-esteem, aggression, child externalising symptoms and attachment problems with peers was found to be associated with mother's permissiveness (Llorca, Richaud & Malonda, 2017). When adolescents had permissive mothers and fathers who were authoritarian, it predicted externalising behaviours and suicidal attempts among adolescents, but, with authoritarian mothers and permissive fathers, it resulted in aggressive behaviours (Zaborskis et al., 2016; Rinaldi & Howe, 2012). Physical aggression and delinquency in girls was found when both parents were permissive (Hoeve et al., 2011).

Authoritarian parenting was found to be associated with children being anxious, having lower emotional regulation and psychological flexibility, making them vulnerable to stressful conditions (Williams, Ciarrochi, & Heaven, 2012). These children were susceptible to externalising and internalising problems, aggression, and were vulnerable to eating disorders and OCD (La Torre-Cruz, Garcia-Linares & Casanova-Arias, 2014; Enten & Golan, 2009). These children were more likely to report depressive symptoms and scored higher on depersonalization and anxiety (Eun, Paksarian, He & Merikangas, 2018; Mousavi, Low & Hashim, 2016; King,

Vidourek & Merianos, 2016). Authoritarian parenting style was also identified to make adolescents susceptible to school misconduct, substance use, delinquent behaviour, bullying and cyberbullying (Zurcher et al., 2018; Rajendran, Kruszewski & Halperin, 2016; Martinez, Fuentes, Garcia & Madrid, 2013).

Children of uninvolved parents seemed to have the poorest outcome. Adolescents raised in uninvolved families used maladaptive achievement strategies, and scored lower on self-esteem (Milevsky et al., 2008). Uninvolved parenting style was also connected with worse substance use outcomes (Luyckx et al., 2011). These adolescents also showed increased antisocial behaviour, exhibited internalising problems, childhood depressive symptoms, and were susceptible to suicidal attempts (Mannarini et al., 2018; Zaborskis et al., 2016; Donath, Graessel, Baier, Bleich & Hillemacher, 2014). Uninvolved parenting was also related to specific eating disorder symptoms like need for thinness, bulimia and body dissatisfaction (Jauregui, Bolanos & Garrido, 2011). Moreover, uninvolved parenting was associated with high delinquency in boys, and the same was found to be lowest in families having at least one authoritative parent (Hoeve et al., 2011).

Role modelling as a part of parenting can help establish appropriate structure leading to good study habits as well. Parental monitoring can range from complete neglect to overprotective pattern where a parent reads for the child. Gaining an insight into this important factor can help counsellors in parent counselling. All these factors ultimately influence the students' academic performance

Academic performance generally refers to how well a student is accomplishing his or her task and studies, but there are quite a number of factors that determine the level and quality of students' academic performance (Stumm et.al, 2011). Many students do badly academically, due to factors other than low intellectual capacity. One such factor can be parenting styles. The two dimensions of parenting styles (i.e. parental warmth and responsiveness) are effective approaches when children are in distress (Dittman et al., 2011). Hence, it can be endorsed that both home environment and parenting styles are effective predictors of academic performance in children. Yet another factor is poor study habits, which often result in poor academic performance even among the naturally bright students. Habits are true indicators of individuality in a person. So study habits are the behaviour of an individual related to studies. In the process of learning, learner's habitual ways of exercising and practicing their abilities for learning are considered as study habits of learners. Understanding the study habits can largely help a counsellor to deal with the problem of underachievement and lack of motivation. (Yazdani & Godbole, 2011)

Study Habits

Learning is a highly complex problem in Psychology. Mace (2002) pointed out that study is a systematic acquisition of knowledge and an understanding of facts and principles that calls for retention and application. Kelly (1998) stated that study is the application of one's mental capacity to the acquisition, understanding and organization of knowledge. Studies require time spent in a deliberate attempt to learn. It should be differentiated from simple leisure to conscious reading-learning. The task of learning is not dependent on the teacher alone. It is not only teacher's responsibility but also the responsibility of the students. Efficient learning depends not only on good teaching but also on satisfactory learning procedures. Efficient learning depends upon the learner's ability to schedule his time, the plan of his study, the habit of concentration, note-taking, mental-review, over learning, the judicious application of whole and part method, massed and distributed learning and so on. In other words, learning involves the development of proper study habits and skills. Crede and Kuncel (2008) defines study habit as study routines consisting of frequency of studying sessions, review of material, self-testing, rehearsal of learned material, and studying in a conducive environment. Additionally, students' attitudes toward the act of studying are referred to as 'study attitudes'. There are many factors affecting study orientation like individual differences, effective usage of time, note-taking, study habits training, teacher, family, proper study environment, homework, using library, reading-listening and writing. However, interest and will are very important for study habits and attitudes. When study habits are analysed in terms of control focus it is revealed that students who have inner control do not need to be controlled too often externally when they undertake an assignment, but students who are controlled with outer factors need guidance and encouragement seemingly often (Bacanli, 2002). Grace (2013) maintains that the most effective process for studying involves highly active behaviour over a period of time, wherein, to study effectively, one must read, draw, compare, memorize and test himself over time. Kelli (2009) posits that for students to succeed in their studies, they must be able to properly integrate course content, comprehend it, reflect on it and be able to articulate the information in written and/or oral form. Developing good time management skills is a very important study habit. Students must realize and be able to prioritise that there is a time to be in class, a time for study, time for family, time to socialize and time for leisure. The critical issue is recognition that there must be an appropriate balance. Students should also have a vision because a clearly articulated picture of the future they intend to create for themselves is very important and contributes to students' success in school. This will promote a passion for what they wish to do. Passion is critical and leads to an intense interest, dedication and commitment to achieving career goals and objectives. Ashish (2013) opines that knowing exactly what does and does not work on a personal level, even tracking ones study patterns and correlating it with related grades and then proactively creating a study plan and schedule around the proven effective methods, is the most powerful study tool of all. The utilization of study skills and habits can play a positive role in improving academic performance of students. Academic achievement and achieving educational goals require the existence of several factors, the most important of which is the study habits of individuals, since the use of varied and effective methods of study improves academic performance of students (Alimohamadi, Dehghani & Saeide, 2018). Hence, the problem of study habit is one of immense importance both from the theoretical and the practical points of view.

The first study habits inventory was developed by Wrenn (1934). His selection of items was based upon the responses of the high achieving and the low achieving students who were matched with regard to their intelligence and major fields of study. An item analysis by Wrenn and Humber was tried in 1941 which resulted in the revision of the original inventory. Correlation between Wrenn's Revised Study habits inventory and scholastic achievement was reported to be quite significant (r = 0.42).

Another self-rating scale of fifty six statements was constructed by Locke (1940). Correlations between scores in Locke's student skill's inventory and one semester grades ranged from 0.07 to 0.39, with a median value of 0.28. Wittenborn, Larsen and Mogils (1945) attempted to correlate the various indices of academic performance with student's reports on study practices for which he used two similar questionnaires. Bi-serial correlation coefficients were computed for the 30 significant items in each questionnaire. It was observed that a large number of study habits were related to the criteria.

Carter (1950) administered two study method tests to several educational psychology classes totalling 800 students. He compared the study habit scores with objective mid-term examination grades and composite measures of achievement. The correlations ranged from 0.33 to 0.49 and 0.46 to 0.51 respectively. Later, Carter's study methods test was administered again in 1951. The correlation with mid-term test scores was 0.40 and with the senior year grade point averages was 0.60. Diener (1960) in an attempt to observe the similarities and differences between overachieving and under-achieving students, also observed that the two groups differed significantly in respect to their study habits. The over-achieving males had better study habits. Insignificant correlation have been reported by Brooks and Heston (1945) between intelligence (ACE scores) and study habits (r = .067). Jamuar (1974) in his thesis concluded that study habit is related to scholastic achievement and affects it independently of intelligence. The National Assessment of Educational Progress (NAEP) in 1994 conducted a study to find out the relationship between study habits and academic performance of students. The study revealed a positive correlation between study habits and academic achievement.

Study habit is an indispensable aspect of the learning process. Effective study habits result in positive learning outcomes while faulty study habits result in poor learning outcomes. Gardner (1978) defined study habits as behaviours that are associated with learning. The term "study habit" refers to a well-planned and deliberate patterns of study which has attained a form of consistency on the part of the student towards understanding academic subjects and passing at examination (Bashir & Mattoo, 2012). Khurshid, Tanveer and Qasmi (2012) said that study habit is, buying out a dedicated scheduled and uninterrupted time to apply one's self to the task of learning. According to Goods dictionary of education, 'study habit is the tendency of pupil to study when the opportunities are provided, the pupil's way of studying whether systematic or unsystematic, efficient or inefficient (Chand, 2013). It is also defined as "strategies of work". Study habit is thus a process by which an adolescent can fulfil his thirst for knowledge (Premalakshmi, 2012).

Different students have different and unique study habits. In the opinion of Katelyn (2013), there is no doubt that different people study in different ways and it may be that what works for one person may not work for another. John (2010) opines that not all students are alike. There are several key study habits that are crucial to all students' success. One such habit is studying in a good environment, with a little bit of background music, such as classical or soft music with no lyrics and a good studying location which is consistent at all study periods. Generally, study habits can be classified into two, good study habits and bad study habits. Good study habits according to Katelyn (2013) are referred to as positive or productive study habits. They are those satisfying study habits which have the tendency to improve the academic performance of students. Good study habits occur as a result of practice and knowing what methods are most effective for oneself as a student. While studying, it is important to manage temptations by staying away from distractions like computer, phone, tablet, I-Pad, play-stations, and etc. Working on a long term assignment daily by studying a little each night, instead of studying the night before can help to avoid procrastination.

A primary tip for developing better study habits involves reviewing what you learnt in class every day after reaching home and recognising the way that works for oneself, this will help one to be successful in studies. Katelyn (2013) therefore, identifies fourteen positive or good study habits which students can employ in order to improve their academic performance. They are: attending all classes, reviewing notes every day, reading material prior to it being covered in class, studying daily, having at least one conference with the professor, developing a word list for the course, reading materials to improve background knowledge of the course (other than text), attending help sessions, attending learning resource lab when available, developing a list of possible questions, asking questions in class, studying an old exam, avoiding a last minute cram session, and sleeping at least 8 hours the night before exams commence. In the same strain, Harpe and Row (2009), highlight good study habits as following: studying every day, creating a quiet place at home or anywhere to study, turning off the phone, TV and other devices that may disturb while studying, listening to soft music or white noise, studying in a way that suits ones learning style, taking regular breaks, not studying at the last minute, studying the hard things first and spending more time on topics one finds difficult, asking for help if one is struggling, taking notes as one studies and organizing notes in a notebook or folder.

On the other hand, bad study habits according to John (2010) are negative or non-productive study habits which are undesirable and counter-productive to students' academic performance. Bad study habits generally range from procrastination, truancy, not taking notes, selective reading, studying while watching television or what is generally regarded as distractive study. Nikki (2013) identified bad study habits which included studying with friends, listening to loud music, studying in uncomfortable conditions and cramming. There are several factors that tend to affect students' study habits. Their ability to study and concentrate can be increased by finding a quiet place where they can concentrate. Distractions such as phones, chat rooms, text messaging, TV, video games, music and computers can all decrease students' ability to learn. Whatever is going on around and within a student's own mind also affects their study habits.

According to research study by SheeRa (2012), study habits can be affected by following factors: age of a student, home environment, studying materials, television and computer games, social networking sites (face book), students' determination and aspiration, financial and economic status of parents, the school rules , the teaching style of teachers, the leisure time activities of the students, availability of library, the friends and peer group, assignments and homework restriction, students' parents educational background, parents not interested and supportive in helping their children study, household chores, family problems, procrastination and poor time management, students' comfort level, the noise level and the lighting level and the availability of items that might be necessary to study or to enhance concentration. The current research likewise attempts to understand study habits and the impact of parenting on it, which in turn will help us grasp and comprehend current trends and their influence on study habits.

Similarly, Hills and Ballow (2000) also developed a comprehensive study skill manual for college students. According to them, effective study cannot be acquired without the application of these skills and methods, some of which include reading, note-taking, time consideration, organizing material in a study and choosing a good study environment among others. The detailed description of their skills are as follows:

Environment of study

Environment is considered to be an important aspect because the place where one studies has an important effect on one's efficiency as the location and all of its characteristics become stimuli. The stimulus of the study situation should produce the response of studying and no other response. It has been suggested that a study room should be well ventilated, noise free and well lighted room or open place with a desk and a chair. Ruch (1995) wrote about the type of chair and desk to be considered for study, wherein it was emphasized that these should be such that allow the individual to maintain an erect and comfortable seating posture. The study desk should be spacious enough for the books and materials, but should contain only what one needs at a time. Hepher (1990) revealed that the effect of temperature and humidity on the body temperature of the individual can cause a reduction in the body function and mechanism. Hence, the emphasis here is on the need for abundance of fresh air in the study environment to avoid unnecessary fatigue.

Hills and Ballow (2000) pointed out that glaring light could cause eye strain and headaches. Therefore covered light bulbs and light coloured blotters can be used to reduce light intensity. Light should not shine directly on the table or reading desk. Taking to consideration a rural setting where students have to study under locally made lamps and hurricane lanterns, these should be adjusted well enough to reduce light intensity or place at a considerable distance away from the reading desk. It has been observed that some people cannot study without music, Hills and Ballow (2000) agree that music is good if it does not constitute noise in itself or when used to neutralize other external noise.

Time Planning

Determining time limits for study sets the immediate goal for completing ones work within specific time limits and also helps one to resist recreational distraction (Robinson, 1990). Hills and Ballow (2000) suggest the use of work diary which allows the student to look at everything he has to do and to apportion time to every subject. Organizing time in this way helps to minimize worry and indecision that may arise in case of any extra work that has to be slotted in. The diary should be planned on the basis of needs and purposes, allocating adequate time to each task so that no particular task consume more time than necessary.

Effective and fast reading

Quick readers take in and retain more than slow readers because the quick reader catches the drift and flow of the passage better, whereas slow readers delay over each word. Solomon (1999) stated that most poor readers were often concerned with unimportant details while the good and fast readers often adopt a wider view of the entire passage. There are some cases in which slow reading can however be adopted depending on the subject matter and the purpose of reading.

Concentration

The ability to direct one's attention on the task at hand is necessary for effective study. Robinson (1990) outlined five major conditions that affect concentration, these include -distractions, (internal and external situations) associated with other activities, study materials not convenient, poor lightening and physiological conditions. Personal problems that keep on flashing to one's mind if not properly tackled and discarded can act as greatest hindrance to concentration.

Comprehension

Robinson (1990) stated that reading with one's head instead of one's eyes is what effective study habit involves. The student must learn to read with an active attitude of seeking what is important in the material. Many students do not seek to understand the basic concepts that seem simple and relevant, but later in their studies, they realize that without learning the basics adequately comprehension of more difficult materials is difficult.

Remembering

It is thought that in remembering, a memory trace is laid down on the mind. And being a sensory impression, by repetition, the traces are made deeper and therefore are more lasting (Hallas, 2002). According to Oladele (2000), there are four kinds of remembering and they include recognition, recall, reproduction and performance. He held the view that our failure to recall emanates from non-practice Furthermore, he maintained that performance, a fourth kind of remembering, is also the performance of habits, so well learned, that they are highly automatic.

Note taking

This is one of the activities that is believed to aid learning and remembering, and consequently academic success Note-taking when properly done, involves not only reading and writing or listening to lectures and jotting down points but also requires concentration and reading for necessary facts.

Arora (2016) suggests that learners who do not have enough information about study strategies do not attain effective and stable learning, and therefore will not have an appropriate level of academic achievement. In other words, students with better academic achievement use these skills more than those with lower academic achievement (Rezaie, Seyed, Reza, Chehrzad & Kazem, 2017). Khan (2016) described poor study habits as the most important reason for students' academic failure. Students with poor academic performance, thereby utilizing the proper skills and study habits, can improve their academic performance and consequently prevent the emergence of educational problems. Understanding the important role of study skills in a student's academic achievement, recently, many prestigious universities such as York University in Canada and University of Berkeley in California teach study skills to newly-enrolled students (Nourian, Shah & Mousavi, 2011). Hence, understanding study habits and factors influencing it, in detail, is crucial for aiding academic progress of students.

According to Robbins et al. (2004), motivation is an important but insufficient condition to perform well in university. He concluded that it is important to include study skills, along with psychosocial variables, in models predicting achievement. Self-regulation is a specifically important skill in the university environment, where students must regulate their own study behaviour. Therefore, study habits are of great assistance to actualize the capacities of the adolescents. A meta-analysis of the Motivated Strategies for Learning Questionnaire (MSLQ) by Crede and Phillips (2011) in their study concluded that of all learning strategies included in the MSLQ, effort regulation, time and study environment management had the highest observed validities for predicting GPA. Additionally, Wintre et al. (2011) reported that first-year students who maintained their secondary school GPA in the first year of higher education had better time management skills than those whose GPA would drop. Hurtado et al. (2007) found that students' time management skills was a noteworthy predictor of academic adjustment. Abott-Chapman, Hughes and Wyld (1992) found that students with insufficient study skills were at risk of academic adjustment problems. A research study by Ebele and Olofu (2017) in Nigeria with 1050 senior secondary school students revealed that there is a significant relationship between study habits and students' academic performance. McDaniel, Howard, and Einstein (2009) are of the opinion that the most common challenge to the success of students is lack of effective or positive study habits. They further maintain that if students can develop a good study habit and follow it up with good discipline, they are bound to perform extraordinarily well in their academic engagements. Husain (2000) stresses that lack of effective or positive study habits, is an acute study problem among students at all levels. Hence, the level of preparation and learning strategies, developed and employed consciously by students influence their level of academic performance to a large extent.

Some psychologists have tried to investigate, whether study habits could be improved through training. Burnett and Collins (1951) illustrated the extent to which the students taking the how-to-study course at Fresno state college increased their cumulative grade point averages. Out of 24 students, 19 made a mean gain of +.25 on a cumulative grade point basis; 5 had a loss of .27. The gain in cumulative grade point for the age group was +.14. Six students raised their grade points more than +.37 in two semesters. Bamman (1954) found statistically significant increment in the test-retest performance of 152 "study skills programme" students on the "Iowa silent reading test" and on the "Co-operative C-2 reading comprehension test" as compared with the results obtained on sixty control subjects. Shaw (1955) studied 153 students who were enrolled in a study-skills course. Before enrolment in a study-skills programme, the students had a mean grade equivalent to C. After study skills training, the weighted mean grade was slightly better than an average C grade.

A study by Chowdhury and Ghose (2014) enumerated that, building up the right attitude to study among adolescents can be a result of parental activities, behaviour, thinking, personality, their interpersonal relationships etc. The child-rearing pattern of the parents is an important factor in achieving good study habits. In particular, parents need to express realistic expectations from their children, so that the latter can find true goals for their studies. When parents are accessible, approachable and the interpersonal relationship of parent and child is guided by clear reason, then the adolescents strive towards educational achievement. It shows that study habits are indeed much affected by parenting. Parents need to be emotionally close to their children and need to be realistic in their approach for their child's study. Leaving the house for non-essential social engagements while telling the child to study is a mark of poor parenting and can't imbibe good study habit among children. Incessant nagging related to study causes resentment in the child. Last but not the least a well-adjusted family life, devoid of too much conflict, sustains the calming atmosphere necessary for good study.

Effective usage of time means reaching objectives within the given time since a person began to study. Deficiency of effective time management is one of the most significant problems of study habits (Glenn, 2003). Cusimano (1999) emphasizes that effective time management is very important for success. The first step of effective time management is making a plan and conforming to it (Ulug, 2000). According to a study by Zeyrek (1990) on students between the ages of 16-21, only 18% have positive features in terms of organization and planning.

Note taking is another important dimension of study habits. Students who use proper study habits containing note taking and studying that notes, can remember the knowledge for longer time (Eliot, Foster & Stinson, 2002). Oguz (1999), found a significant difference between the students who received note-taking training, were encouraged to taking notes and reviewing them as opposed to students who attended classes without receiving note-taking training. Studies point out that effective note-taking increases students' success in class (Austin, Lee & Carr, 2003). However, many students prefer to take the notes from their friends making it difficult to learn note taking for themselves (Wolff, 2001).

Motivation

Motivation is defined as internal condition that stimulates, directs and maintains behaviour. There is a strong relationship between learning and motivation. According to Maslow (1970) when the need for love and belongingness are fulfilled, individual can then concentrate on higher level needs of intellectual achievement (Woolfolk, 2004). Achievement motivation can best be understood by exploring the implications of "achievement" and "motivation" separately. Achievement is the importance of accomplishment and fulfilment with effort involved (Mandel & Marcus, 1988). Motivation is an individual's need for engaging in an activity, that is, the degree to which an individual chases the activity as well as the determination of the individual (Graham & Weiner, 1996). According to Deci and Ryan (2000) motivation is greatly appreciated because of the consequences it produces. The attitude that is often used along with motivation to achieve is self-concept, that is the way one thinks about oneself to perform a task successfully. Research evidence supports the contention that positive academic self-concept contributes to academic achievement by enhancing the motivation to achieve.

Motivating students so that they can succeed in school is one of the greatest challenges of this century. Lack of motivation is a huge hurdle in learning and a pertinent cause in the weakening of education standards (Awan, Noureen & Naz, 2011). Baker and Siryk (1984) categorised academic adjustment into four aspects, which are motivation to learn and having clear academic goals, applying oneself to academic work, exerting effort to meet academic demands and being satisfied with the academic environment. Research by Bailey and Phillips (2016) also showed that academic adjustment influences academic achievement. As motivation to learn is one of the key factors, understanding motivation with regards to achievement becomes important. According to McClelland (1985), achievement motivation has been defined as the amount of individual difference in the need to attain rewards, such as physical contentment, feelings of personal mastery, and seeking praise. The theory of achievement motivation is concerned with the interaction of personality and the immediate environment as a determinant of aspiration, efforts and persistence, when an individual expects that performance will be evaluated as success or failure, in relation to some standard of excellence.

One of the most prominent figures in motivation research, David McClelland, began his work on the subject as early as the 1940s. The modern study of achievement motivation began with the work of David McClelland. He and his associates devised the term 'n Ach' representing need for achievement (McClelland, 1961; McClelland & Winter, 1969). This theory suggests that under suitable conditions, people will repeat doing what they have been earlier rewarded for doing. Need for Achievement (nAch) is one of the psychological motives that play a crucial role in success and achievements of a man. People who strive for excellence in a field for the sake of achieving and not for some reward are considered to have a high need for achievement. So the need for achievement or n-Ach was defined as the desire or tendency to do things rapidly and to accomplish something difficult to master, manipulate, organize, or create new ideas. And, in addition, do things rapidly and independently as possible, to overcome obstacles and obtain a high standard, to excel oneself and surpass others, and to increase self-regard (Murray, 1938). McClelland also studied the strength of power motivation and affiliation motivation that individuals exhibit within groups or organizations. Power motivation might be exhibited in educational settings by students who are extremely competitive, who attain a sense of power by being recognized as the brightest student or as the student most likely to succeed. Affiliation motivation is displayed in response to a longing for approval in social contexts, for example, in situations where a student receives praise for doing well from family or friends. Motivation as an academic engagement refers to "cognitive, emotional, and behavioral indicators of student investment in and attachment to education" (Tucker, Zayco & Herman, 2002).

Another significant jump in motivational studies is goal orientation theory. The basic premise of achievement goal orientation theory is that students set many personal goals when they involve in academic tasks and the kinds of goals that students embrace can directly affect their academic outcomes (Elliot & McGregor, 2001). Achievement goal orientation can be stated as individuals' personal beliefs, established to arrange their skills or to reveal the goals set out to be successful (Ames, 1992), and as personal perceptions about the reasons for learning and focusing on goals for being successful (Kaplan & Maehr, 2007; Pintrich, 2000). This theory reveals the reasons behind student performance while performing classroom activities, learning formations and academic tasks. At the same time, achievement goal orientation theory focuses on what the students think while recognising goals in any situations. In fact, the desire to succeed and to avoid failure motivates individuals (Middleton & Midgley, 1997). In this context, it can be said that achievement goal orientation also has an effect on influencing students' school behaviours (Buluş, 2011). Although there are different types of achievement goal orientation, they can be incorporated into two broad categories: performance goal orientation and learning goal orientation.

Performance Goal Orientation focuses on displaying skills by taking others as references, and is based on proving ability or avoidance of feeling incompetent (Jagacinski & Duda, 2001). Performance goal orientation has undesirable outcomes such as unwillingness to ask for academic support (Ryan & Stiller, 1991), cheating (Anderman, Griesinger & Westerfield, 1998), withdrawal in the face of failure (Dweck & Leggett, 1988) and use of artificial browsing strategies (Greene & Miller, 1996). Students with performance goal orientation feel that it is extremely important to be judged well by others and they avoid being appraised negatively. These individuals are generally extrinsically motivated. They often perceive mistakes as failure and may easily quit what they are studying. These individuals have a tough time facing difficult situations, trying to look competent and making a good impression by putting effort into being successful or avoiding failure (Greene & Miller, 1996). Learning goal orientation is related to student desire to have a complete understanding of the topic and to absorb well in the learning process. Students with learning goal orientation consider skills as equivalent to learning. Here, individuals believe that effort increases the ability to gain skills, and compare their past and current performances to check their development (Schunk, 1996). Those who have learning goal orientation understand that problems do occur and are capable of coping with them. They don't decrease their motivation when they come across difficult situations. They try to do their best and use different cognitive strategies and methods during the learning process (Izci & Koc, 2012).

In reviewing the research literature on the topic of self as it relates to motivation, Maehr and Braskamp (1986) have identified three areas in which self-concept plays a vital role. The three areas are self-consistency, self-confidence, and self-determination. Recent work on self-determination has pointed to the importance of cultivating a sense of ownership or of control over a situation before individuals will become motivated to act (Decharms & Richard, 1984). In a school setting, a sense of self-determination could well be a critical element in engendering motivation among students.

Elliot and McGregor's (2001) model of achievement motivation, describes two main types of goals: mastery goals meaning to "master" the task at hand, and performance goals; i.e. - demonstrating higher performance in relation to others. Research indicates that when students take on mastery goals, they engage in effective cognitive processing strategies (Noar, Anderman, Zimmerman & Cupp, 2005). Social goals are another vital type of goals, although they have not been examined at length, as have mastery and performance goals (Dowson & McInerney, 2001). In these goals, social reasons make a person to try to achieve in academics. According to Maehr (2008) achievement motivation is psycho-social by nature. It does occur in groups, where interpersonal interactions can either weaken or facilitate commitment towards the tasks to be done.

Hence, it is important both for parents and educators to understand - why promoting and encouraging achievement motivation from an early age is imperative. It is a consistent, striving force of an individual to achieve success to certain standard of excellence, within the competing situation. The students form self-concept, values and beliefs about their abilities at a young age in school. The development of early academic achievement motivation has significant implications on later academic careers. A great deal of research has found that students with high achievement motivation are more likely to have increased levels of academic achievement, and have lower dropout rates (1997). According to Alschuler (1973), most students tend to fall somewhere in the middle of the achievement scale between extremely high achievers and, those who may not achieve at all. Everyone has a need to achieve and a fear of failure, but these needs vary from person to person, and from situation to situation. Each student operates from different levels of motivation they have developed, however, some students are predisposed to have little to no desire to accomplish certain tasks (Atkinson, 1999). Using a simple test designed by Atkinson and Feather (1966), those students who lack motivation can be identified (McClelland, 1968) and can be worked with independently, to increase their motivation and their productivity (Parker and Johnson, 1981).

Maslow has pointed out towards Intrinsic and Extrinsic motivation.

Intrinsic and Extrinsic Motivation

Intrinsic/extrinsic motivation refers to whether the motivation is stemming more from inside a person or outside of him/her. Intrinsic motivation refers to the motivation which is originated inside a person. There is no reward except the activity itself. It means that the essence of motivated action is the sense of autonomy and the desire is self-initiating and self-regulating. While in extrinsic motivation there is an anticipation of reward from outside, and a person is motivated from an outside source rather than the self. Intrinsic/extrinsic motivation is related to the term 'locus of control' which was first introduced by Rotter (1966).

Maslow (1970) believed that intrinsic motivation is noticeably superior to extrinsic because we are motivated to achieve "self-actualization". Bruner (1966) claimed that one of the most effective ways to help students is to free them from the control of rewards. In some cases, the two kinds of motivation may overlap to some degree because one may be motivated from both an inside source and an outside one at the same time. Generally speaking, both kinds of motivation play important roles in learning, and lack of motivation can cause procrastination because motivation is the driving force that makes people act. In other words, presence of motivation can increase learning behaviour. Research on intrinsic motivation has suggested that a task that possesses a certain optimum level of uncertainty and unpredictability tends to be generally attractive. Although social experiences can reduce the search for novelty, new information, and challenge, it appears that from the start, human beings have a built-in attraction to these features in tasks. Thus, it is likely that schools where the students feel appropriately challenged to be academically successful and where the rewards of learning take the form of problem solving or successfully meeting challenges will have a higher level of motivation among its students. When individuals choose what they want to learn based on their interests and expectations, they have intrinsic motivation to complete tasks. However, when they learn only to get good grades without the need to improve themselves, they will develop extrinsic motivation (Amabile, 1996).

Deci and Ryan (1985), in their model of Self-determination theory (SDT) describe the term 'motivation', as the conscious reason for a behaviour rather than the operant function, which means that it refers to the antecedent reason or expectation of a behaviour rather than the consequences. The primary focus of the model is to differentiate between different sources of motivation and the extent to which they are internalized (Deci, Vallerand, Pelletier & Ryan, 1991). The model describes five types of motivation that are divided into two groups: the intrinsic and integrated types of motivations are called autonomous (i.e., internal) motivation while external and introjected types of motivations are called externally regulated motivation. Depending on the type of motivation, different effects on health behaviours and school work have been observed. For instance, people who report autonomous motivation are more likely to succeed in maintaining health behaviours such as smoking cessation, because they are less dependent on external factors (Ryan & Patrick, 2008). Even though motivation often originates from external sources, SDT states that the process of internalizing motivation for functional behaviours, i.e.:- going from controlled to autonomous motivation is an important factor in explaining the maintenance of behaviour (Hagger & Chatzisarantis, 2009, Markland, Ryan, Tobin & Rollnick, 2005).

To almost any educational psychologist, motivation is one of those things that has been, is and probably always will be at the heart of teaching and learning (Maehr & Meyer, 1997). However adolescent's strong motivation for learning in school diminishes by the early years of adolescence, and poor motivation becomes one of the chief predictors for teenager's low achievement in secondary school (Krause, Boucher & Duchesse, 2003). Thus it is valuable to study adolescent's achievement motivation especially the factors that can affect it.

Brown (2007) reviewed the definitions of motivation based on the three historical schools of thought as follows:

Behaviourism: this perspective sees motivation as the anticipation of reward. Driven to acquire positive reinforcement and based on our prior experience we repeat the action to get rewards.

Cognitivism: it sees motivation as choices people make. The forces behind our decisions are the needs or drives. Ausubel (1968) identified 6 needs for the construct of motivation: the need for exploration, manipulation, activity, stimulation, knowledge, and ego enhancement.

Constructivism: each person is motivated differently and the emphasis is on social context and individual personal choices.

Achievement motivation is an important issue for psychologists and individuals in the field of education because it has been correlated with academic self-concept (Marsh & Ayotte, 2003), academic self-efficacy (Bong & Skaalvik, 2003), personality traits (Mandel & Marcus, 1988), developmental level (Guay, Marsh & Boivin, 2003) and gender differences (Mandel & Marcus, 1988). Achievement motivation is considered a prerequisite for success, not only in academic, but also in sports and job related situations. In academic settings, the interest in motivation is partly inspired by the notion that students' motivation and their competency beliefs and value beliefs, could be more malleable than their cognitive ability, and could prove to be a potential lead for the educational system for improving learning and achievement processes in students (Spinath, Spinath, Harlaar & Plomin, 2006).

An empirical study by Rooij, Jansen and Grift (2017) investigated how intrinsic motivation, academic self-efficacy, self-regulated study behaviour and satisfaction with the chosen degree programme influenced academic adjustment in university, and how these variables and adjustment affected three important indicators of student success: grade point average (GPA), attained number of credits (ECTS) and intention to persist. Results showed that academic adjustment was influenced by intrinsic motivation, self-regulated study behaviour and degree programme satisfaction, which together explained 72% of the variance in adjustment. Motivational and behavioural variables did not influence GPA and credits directly, but did influence through academic adjustment. Additionally, only satisfaction with the degree programme predicted intention to persist. These results point to the importance of academic adjustment in predicting university GPA and credits, and the pivotal role of satisfaction with the degree programme in predicting intention to persist. The construct of academic adjustment can be summarised by successful interaction between a first-year student, and the academic characteristics and demands of the university environment. A student enters higher education with certain personal characteristics like personality, motivation, study skills, which change upon interaction with the new educational environment. Successful interaction with this new environment, such as having positive interactions with lecturers and peers, and being able to handle the increased complexity, and quantity of the learning content, then determines whether or not a student is satisfied with the first-year experience and whether he or she gets good grades, and persists to the second year (Astin, 1999; Pascarella & Terenzini, 2005; Sevinç & Gizir, 2014). Prior literature consistently showed the crucial role of academic adjustment in predicting achievement (Aspelmeier, Love, McGill, Elliott & Pierce, 2012; Rienties, Beausaert, Grohnert, Niemantsverdriet & Kommers, 2012; Wintre et al., 2011) and persistence in higher education (Kennedy, Sheckley & Kehrhahn, 2000; Kuh, Kinzie, Buckley, Bridge & Hayek, 2006). Lowe and Cook (2003) found that 20 to 30% of university students experienced considerable difficulty adjusting to higher education, leading a significant number to drop out or underachieve.

Bulus (2011) shared that achievement goal orientation changes students' behaviours at school and their use of different learning strategies (Izci & Koc, 2012). These differences in consequence affect students' academic success. Yazdani and Godbole (2014) from their research concluded that achievement motivation and study habits tend to have a positive effect on academic performance of students and helped them better performance and academic achievement.

Many of the researchers have concluded that students' achievement motivation have positive impact upon their scores, and subject's achievement motivation enables them to be more organized in their studies (Abouserie, 1995; Akbaş & Kan 2007; Tella, 2007). In a nutshell, achievement motivation contributes to enhance achievement level. Therefore, it could be suggested that motivation has an important effect on academic achievement, and also is an important component of educational and instructional processes. Hence, the following research focuses on understanding more about this important factor of achievement motivation.

To develop effective study habits and motivation it is important that one deals with stressful situations that may arise, effectively. This is determined by our coping strategies.

Coping with stress

Coping can be broadly viewed as a psychological mechanism that creates ways for finding an adequate response to environmental demands and challenges. According to Lazarus and Folkman (1984), coping is conceptualized as an effort to manage stressful demands, and is a goal-oriented process owing to cognitive control mechanisms. In the course of primary appraisal, the person evaluates how much and what environmental influences are important to him/her, if they are of concern, or promise him/her some benefits. During the secondary appraisal, the person raises a personal question, of whether he/she needs to do anything at all. If the answer is 'yes', then further questions arise: what is the given demand, what he/she can do, what is about to happen and what will influence his/her well-being (Lazarus & Folkman, 1984, Lazarus, 1991).

There are three options: a) harm/loss is an appraisal a person makes if he/she has in the past lived through something which could not be changed; b) threat is an appraisal which is made when a person presumes that he/she might get hurt or expect a loss in the future; c) challenge is an appeal for effort, for utilising coping resources. An experience with a perceived threatening stimuli arouses negative emotions and these block a person's functioning. When a person evaluates the situation as being beyond one's ability to cope with demands because of lack of resources, the result is stress (Lazarus & Folkman, 1984). To summarize, coping is an individual's adaptation to the environment, meaning an individual's efforts to maintain control over events in the best realistic possible ways.

Coping is defined as "constantly altering cognitive and behavioural attempts to manage specific external and/or internal demands that are appraised as taxing or exceeding the resources of the person" (Lazarus & Folkman, 1984). Different ways of coping are as follows: Problem solving, Cognitive restructuring, Social support, Express emotions, Problem avoidance, Wishful thinking and Social withdrawal.

Lazarus and Folkman (1984) provided a broad model of coping that has guided research for over two decades and they posited that coping is distinguished between problem-focused (i.e., acting on the problem) and emotion-focused responses (i.e., acting on one's emotions). Although this conceptual model shaped the field of coping and continues to guide current research, the categories in this organization of coping responses have been criticized for not being conceptually clear, exhaustive, or mutually exclusive

(Skinner, Edge, Altman & Sherwood, 2003). Skinner et al. recommended that not only should this model of coping be no longer used, but also argued that any bottom up, exploratory approach to the structure of coping (e.g., problem-focused vs. emotion-focused) is problematic, as it capitalizes on idiosyncrasies of the study sample and contributes to inconsistencies in the literature. Consequently, Skinner et al. noted the need for future research to organize coping responses around top-down, theory-driven categories.

Connor-Smith, Compas, Wadsworth, Thomsen, and Saltzman (2000) posited a top-down, dual process model of responses to stress that distinguishes between automatic responses (i.e., stress reactivity) and voluntary responses (i.e., coping). Confirmatory factor analysis (CFA) of the conceptual model divided automatic stress responses into two broader constructs of involuntary engagement (i.e., rumination, intrusive thoughts, emotional arousal, physiological arousal, and impulsive action) and involuntary disengagement (i.e., inaction, emotional numbing, involuntary avoidance, and cognitive interference). These involuntary reactions are rooted in an individual's temperament and develop prior to the conscious, controlled responses. Further, CFA supported three distinct coping categories: primary control, secondary control, and disengagement coping. Specifically, primary control coping refers to efforts to act directly on a problem or one's emotions through problem-solving, emotional modulation, or emotional expression; secondary control coping refers to efforts to adapt to the problem through acceptance, positive thinking, cognitive reappraisal, or distraction; lastly, disengagement coping represents efforts to evade the problem or one's emotions through denial, avoidance, or wishful thinking. Notably, this conceptual model of stress responses has successfully been confirmed and validated in both child and adult samples, clinical and community samples, as well as cross-culturally (Compas et al., 2006a, 2006b; Compas, Connor-Smith, Saltzman, Thomsen & Wadsworth, 2001; Yao, 2010).

Taken as a whole, research has shown that the primary control and the secondary control coping strategies are generally more adaptive than disengagement coping in response to stressors. Specifically, it has been shown that primary control coping is related to fewer psychological symptoms in the context of controllable stressors (e.g., academic stressors) while secondary control coping has consistently been shown to be associated with better adjustment in response to uncontrollable stressors (e.g., parental depression).

Utilizing effective coping strategies can help alleviate the negative effects of stress and help in overall adjustment. Adjustment and stress are also important factors influencing study habits and motivation. According to Folkman & Lazarus (1980), coping strategies can be viewed as what an individual actually thinks and does in a particular stressful situation. In general, coping efforts may change constantly for any one individual. Lazarus and Folkman (1984) distinguished between two types of coping strategies: problem-focused and emotion-focused.

- Problem focused coping strategies tend to be employed when an individual has determined that a harmful, threatening, or challenging situation is amenable to change. Thus, the individual who is experiencing stress perceives the stressful situation to be alterable and within his or her capabilities of control. As a result, these strategies focused on managing or altering the situation causing stress.

- In contrast, emotion-focused coping strategies focused on dealing with the negative emotions that are a product of the stressful situation. When the individual who is experiencing stress perceives the stressful situation to be outside of his or her control, emotion focused coping strategies may be employed. In other words, these types of strategies are used when an individual has judged that nothing can be done to modify a harmful, threatening, or challenging environment.
- Renk and Smith (2007) explained third type of coping strategy, avoidance coping, which tends to reduce stress over short periods of time as well as prevents anxiety from becoming crippling when confronting uncontrollable stressors. In addition, avoidance allows for gradual recognition of a threat. Increased hope and courage are possibilities when avoidance strategies are used in a partial, tentative, or minimal manner.

Coping with stress in adolescents depend to a large extent on parents. A number of positive parenting behaviours are thought to be associated with the ways in which children regulate emotions and respond to stress.

First, parents who are sensitive and responsive to their child's emotional experiences are likely to be more aware and accepting of emotions, communicating a message that negative emotions are understandable and can be expressed (Thompson & Meyer, 2007). Further, these parents may engage their children in conversations about how to modulate emotions and cope with stress (Havighurst, Wilson, Harley & Prior, 2009). Second, parents who are positive and effective communicators are thought to be able to engage their children in developmentally appropriate conversations about stress, the role of emotions, and adaptive ways to deal with problems (Gentzler, Contreras-Grau, Kerns & Weimer, 2005). Third, warm/supportive parents likely serve as resources through informational support (e.g., offer concrete ways to cope), emotional support (e.g., comfort and listen), or instrumental support (e.g., problem solve with the child) (Smith, 2006). Further, it is suggested that children of supportive caregivers feel more secure approaching their parents when stressed (Bynum & Brody, 2005) as well as expressing, rather than suppressing, negative emotions (Eisenberg, Spinrad & Eggum, 2010) . Through these salient supportive experiences, children may become more comfortable seeking support from others (e.g., peers & teachers) (McIntyre & Dusek, 1995). Fourth, Grolnik and Farkas (2002) argue that children need opportunities to practice coping strategies, and it is thought that structured and consistent environments create a safe context for children to refine their skills, having confidence in their parents' assistance if needed. In addition, children who feel secure in the parent-child relationship are more likely to actively engage with their environment, and so it is possible that these children rely on more engagement coping strategies (Kliewer, Fearnow & Miller, 1996). Lastly, parents who are positively reinforcing and explaining specifically in their responses may provide their children with more constructive feedback and praise about their skills and efforts at coping.

Studies by Bharadwaj (1995, 1996) indicate that the performance of the child is governed by the various parenting styles in which they are being brought up. It was found that cordial relations with parents showed better social adjustment, emotional adjustment and development of self-esteem, whereas deprivation of occasions to be loved and belonged hinders the development of personality. There is a high degree of self-confidence and non-dependency in a healthy parent-child relationship which then leads to feelings of being loved and accepted. Parental acceptance was found to be positively related to achievement and educational competence. Whereas parental rejection makes children fearful, insecure, attention seeking, jealous, aggressive, hostile and emotionally less stable with poor educational achievement and more aggressive tendencies.

Positive relationship with parents is found to act as a type of social support, thereby enhancing psychological resources. Increased social support helps the adolescents in turn to cope with stressful events (Cohen & Wills, 1985; Baumrind, 1991). Reviews of studies by McKee, Colletti, Rakow, Jones and Forehand, 2008 and McLeod, Weisz and Wood, 2007 suggest that parents who are warm/supportive, responsive, and create a structured family context promote positive psychological adjustment, while parents who are intrusive, withdrawn, and coercive undermine children's psychosocial development. Tam, Chong, Kadirvelu and Khoo (2013) concluded that authoritative parenting style is highly associated with self-efficacy. Results showed that authoritative parenting style contributed to 12.8% towards students' self-efficacy. However, authoritarian and permissive parenting styles did not lead to significant relationship with self-efficacy.

Self-efficacy is a person's perception of the ability to perform adequately in a given situation (Bandura, 1997). Self-efficacy can be in different areas and academic self-efficacy is one of them. Academic self-efficacy is the strongest non-cognitive correlate of GPA. Academic self-efficacy in the university context refers to a student's confidence that he or she can perform adequately in the university environment. Academic self-efficacy also relates to effort and perseverance in learning, self-regulation, less stress in demanding situations and better adjustment to new learning situations (Chemers, Hu & Garcia, 2001). Another research by McKenzie and Schweitzer (2001) showed that the prediction of GPA improved by 12% when academic integration and self-efficacy were added to a model with university entry score as a predictor. Further research by De Clercq, Galand, Dupont and Frenay (2013), who used an inclusive approach that took into account several predictors, also reported that self-efficacy was one of the most powerful predictors of GPA at the end of the first year in university. Willcoxson, Cotter and Joy (2011) found that the opposite of academic self-efficacy that is, lack of academic confidence, caused students to give up their studies. Several studies examining the relationship between academic self-efficacy and adjustment showed that self-efficacy, or the comparable concept of academic self-confidence, positively affected adjustment (Chemers et al., 2001; Martin, Kulstad & Madson, 1999).

Bandura's (1997) self-efficacy theory, also states that people high in efficacy show more persistence in the face of challenges and the transition from secondary education to university is such a challenge. Moreover, Aspelmeier, Love, McGill, Elliott and Pierce (2012) found that self-esteem and internal locus of control had a positive effect on first-year students' academic adjustment. Pintrich (2004) reiterated based on his findings that self-efficacy is an important factor in the transition from secondary to university education due to its influence on behaviour regulation. Self-regulated study behaviour is very important in university because instructors provide little control or structure and more autonomy and responsibility is demanded from the students. These studies do point out the importance of coping strategies with regards to academic success, hence this current research on understanding influence of parenting on study habits, achievement motivation and coping with stress is much needed and will further add to the literature.

Regarding familial and parental factors, parental rejection and overly protective parenting are factors significantly related to anxiety disorder in children (Lieb et al., 2000; Knappe et al., 2009) while parental stress, anxiety, and depression also increased the risk (Barrett, Shortt & Healy,

2002; Moffitt., 1993). Parental rejection and physical punishment leads to negative behavioural adjustment in children like high levels of anxiety, depression and social phobia (Mousavi, Low, & Hashim, 2016). High level of rejection and hostility among fathers was strongly associated with somatisation (Lackner, Gudleski & Blanchard, 2004). Parenting behaviours that included punitive actions like spanking and physical aggression was linked with high levels of child disruptive behaviour problems, aggression and bullying (Zurcher, Holmgren, Coyne, Barlett, & Yang, 2018). Although harsh discipline like verbal and physical punishment was linked with child behaviour problems, parental warmth seemed to cushion the children from the damaging effects of such harsh discipline (Simons & Conger, 2007).

Positive developmental outcomes comprising of good development of inhibition capacities in children was related to warmth and responsiveness. Children of parents who demonstrated low levels of warmth showed high levels of oppositional behaviours (Roskam, Stievenart, Meunier, & Noël, 2014). High maternal care was related to lower probabilities of depression, eating, and behavioural disorders (Eun, Paksarian, He, & Merikangas, 2018), while lack of maternal care resulted in self-handicapping; a cognitive strategy wherein there is avoidance of effort to prevent possible failure from hurting self-esteem (Want & Kleitman, 2006). High paternal care was linked to lower chances of social phobia and alcohol abuse/ dependence (Eun, Paksarian, He & Merikangas, 2018), whereas lack of paternal care lead to impostor feeling, wherein the individual suspects their own accomplishments (Want & Kleitman, 2006).

Apart from positive parenting, a number of negative parenting behaviours are thought to be associated with the specific ways in which children respond to stress. First, children of caregivers who are critical and coercive may be less likely to seek support from their parents in times of need (Shipman & Zeman, 2001). Second, parents who minimize and are insensitive to their children's emotions and difficulties are thought to communicate a message that negative emotions are unacceptable and should not be expressed (Eisenberg, Cumberland & Spinrad, 1998).

Third, parents who respond inconsistently to their children's feelings and behaviours create an unpredictable emotional family climate, limiting their children's willingness to seek guidance and undermining feelings of security in openly discussing and expressing emotions (Thompson & Meyer, 2007). Fourth, parents who are withdrawn and dismissive of their children's problems are not likely to help problem solve or offer specific strategies for coping. Further, these children may not develop self-efficacy in their coping abilities, finding it more immediately reinforcing to suppress emotions and avoid their problems (Eisenberg, Fabes & Murphy, 1996). Fifth, parents who are intrusive in their interactions may not effectively scaffold children's learning of coping strategies or give them appropriate opportunities to practice; moreover, these parents may become easily frustrated, and instead of engaging with the child, they may either give up or try to fix the problem for the child. Lastly, it is likely that negative parenting behaviours exacerbate children's emotional reactivity, making it more difficult for them to learn and use adaptive strategies, thereby increasing the likelihood that they will use avoidance coping to diminish their reactivity (Jaffee, Gullone & Hughes, 2010).

Overprotective parenting style appeared to have an unfavorable effect on children. Overprotection was related to the development of anxiety disorders and was found to be an important mediator of the relationship between maternal trait anxiety and child separation anxiety (Orgiles, Penosa, Morales, Fernández-Martínez, & Espada, 2018). It was also linked to social anxiety, social phobia, pubertal anorexia nervosa, and high depressive symptoms (Orgiles et al., 2018; Albinhac, Jean, & Bouvard, 2018; Mousavi et al., 2016; Faravelli, Di Paola, Scarpato, & Fioravanti, 2010). Mothers of panic disorder adolescents were highly overprotective and controlling (Faravelli et al., 2010), while, paternal overprotection lead to impostor feelings in their children (Want & Kleitman, 2006).

High degree of parental control was associated with problem behaviours in children like aggression, anxiety, and depression. High maternal control was linked to lower levels of perceived competence and externalising symptoms leading to greater chances of depression, anxiety, eating, and behavioural disorders. High paternal control was related to high possibilities of agoraphobia and alcohol abuse/dependence (Affrunti & Ginsburg, 2012).

Excessive parental control affects child's confidence and sense of competence, especially in social situations restricting the child's development of autonomy. High control, along with low guidance by parents was observed to result in extrinsic motivational orientation, and high amounts of anxiety and depression symptoms, and aggression among children (Bronstein, Ginsburg & Herrera, 2005). Parents who exhibited autonomy-supporting behaviour were observed as having children with more intrinsic motivational drive (Rajendran, Kruszewski, & Halperin, 2016).

Thus, a home is a place of acceptance where psychological and physical needs are met. Unfavourable home atmosphere acts as a barrier to acceptance and causes a strain in interpersonal relations. The type of parent-child relation may influence the children classifying them broadly into two groups' i.e.:- accepted and rejected children. Accepted children are those whose physical or verbal needs are satisfied. Physical attention may be shown by hugging, kissing or caring for a child. Verbal affection is shown through encouragements, appreciation and complementing them. All these behavioural patterns are likely to instil in a child, a feeling that he is wanted and accepted.

Rejected children are those who are disliked or disapproved of for no valid reason by their parents. Rejection is manifested in two principal ways i.e. parental hostility / aggression and parental indifference. Hostility / aggression are expressed by hitting, kicking, pushing, beating and pinching a child. Indifference is the lack of concern or interest in the child. These behavioural patterns are likely to make a child feel unloved and rejected. Thus parenting style has a great influence on the personality development and their academic achievement. The above researches also show that parental acceptance is positively related with self-concept, curiosity, cognitive competence and achievement of adolescents. With above understanding of the given factors, the current research was designed.

Objectives

The objectives of the present study are as follows –

(a) To understand the factors of parenting styles, study habits, achievement motivation and coping with stress among adolescent students.

(b) To study the outcome of perceived parenting styles on study habits of adolescents'.

(c) To examine the impact of perceived parenting styles on achievement motivation of adolescents'.

(d) To examine the influence of perceived parenting styles on adolescents' achievement motivation.

(e) To study the relationship between study habits and achievement motivation amongst adolescents.

(f) To find out the impact of different perceived parenting styles on the factor of coping with stress among adolescents.

(g) To understand the effect of different perceived parenting styles on the development of coping strategies of positive reappraisal, problem solving, cognitive avoidance and acceptance or resignation in adolescents.

CHAPTER- II
REVIEW OF LITERATURE

Review of Literature

Family is the setting in which children attain essential skills, such as decision-making, responsibility, being respectful to others, showing affection and receiving love, fulfilling social roles and expressing creativity and start their first education (Dil & Bulantekin, 2011). Brown and Iyengar (2008), from their study concluded that parenting style has an effect on self-efficacy, self-respect, self-development, academic motivation, and the behaviour of the individual. Hence, it is important to understand the influence of parents and environment on child's study habits, motivation and personality. Review of studies on parenting styles and its impact on children provides greater understanding into the influence of parenting process.

A research study by Kuppens and Ceulemans (2019) on 600 families with 8-10 year old children showed that having authoritative parents resulted in most favourable outcomes, while having authoritarian and intrusive parents coincided with the least favourable outcomes. Positive developmental outcomes in youth, such as psychosocial competence (for example, positivity, maturation, resilience, self-esteem, self-sufficiency, social competence) and academic achievement have been related to authoritative parenting style (Steinberg, Lamborn, Darling, Mounts & Dornbusch, 1994). Permissive/ indulgent parenting has been inconsistent and showing associations with internalizing (for example, anxiety, depression, withdrawn behaviour, somatic complaints) and externalizing problem behaviour (for example, school misconduct and delinquency).

Negative developmental outcomes, such as aggression, delinquency, somatic complaints, depersonalization and anxiety has been linked with authoritarian parenting style (Williams et al., 2009). Hoeve et al. (2008) shared that least favourable consequences like lack of self-regulation and social responsibility, poor school competence, poor self-sufficiency and social competence, delinquency, anxiety, depression and somatic complaints were found in children of neglectful parents.

Elias and Yee (2009), from their study shared that majority of the students perceived both paternal and maternal parenting style as authoritative, that is, they felt that when their parents, both father and mother provide clear and firm direction, when their parents are rational in setting up rules for them then they can respect and follow them clearly.

Furthermore, some culture specific research was conducted by Keshavarz and Baharudin (2009), which stated that Malaysian parents, regardless of races, endorsed authoritarian parenting and it is well accepted locally. This is because Malaysia is one of the collectivist country where children are taught to conform to group's rules, behave in socially acceptable manner, inhibit own needs and be considerate over others within the group, which, in this context is to obey parents. Similarly, Indian adolescents' perceive their fathers as demanding, which is exhibited by fewer verbal communications between the father and the child. Lesser frequency of verbalization by fathers and more emphasis on imposing consequences rather than verbal resolution are being stated as the plausible reasons behind adolescents' perception of their fathers as demanding (D'souza & Mendes, 2014). However, another research by Saraswathi and Ganapathy (2002) shows that Indian parents are now encouraging autonomy, leading to individualistic orientation, increasing parent-child interaction and thus adding to greater self-sufficiency and adaptation among their children. There is yet another study talking about changing nature of Indian parenting, which enumerates that adolescents' perception of paternal responsiveness was found to significantly predict strategic coping in adolescents. Recent investigation demonstrates that middle class urban fathers of India are turning out to be more affectionate, and nurturing towards their children, pointing to a cultural shift (Roopnarine, Talukder, Jain, Joshi & Srivastav, 1990).

Results of research by Lin and Lian (2011) showed that mothers preferred authoritative parenting as compared to fathers. There was found to be no gender difference in adolescents' coping styles. McKinney and Renk (2008), in their research paper elaborated on gender differences in parenting between mother and father. According to them, psychoanalytic theory contends that mothers are primary attachment figure for children leading to them being close to mothers in their initial years. Further, the gender and role theory attributes differences in child rearing to male and female qualities with the traditional mothers' role as loving and caring figures and fathers assuming the role of authority figure and the provider for family.

A study shows that there is a positive influence of better parental education on achievement-motivation of adolescents (Acharya & Joshi,

2009). Lola and Shrinidhi (2008) found that academic achievement of children is affected by parenting styles and also by parental education. Parents who have a high level of education tend to be more authoritative, showing that parental education influences the behavioural style adopted by parents. Ekeke and Telu (2013), recommended that, good parents provide their children the advantages that they actually need for their school, career, and then in turn children develop proper aims and goals of future life.

Nei (1965) found that, faulty environment produces faulty learning. Every family does not carry out its task of socialization with equal effectiveness. Thus, that child is a product of his/her family environment and it is the nature of the home he/she comes from that determines the nature of the child to a great extent. Muller and Kerbow (1993) in their research found that parental involvement with and monitoring of homework is related to adolescent's completion of homework. Clark (1993) in his research paper found that parents of children who monitor their children's behaviour after school were more likely to have high achieving children.

Results from a study correlating the parenting styles with academic achievement showed that there is positive relationship between authoritative parenting style and academic achievement while permissive parenting was negatively associated with academic achievement of adolescents (Elham, Siti, Rumaya & Mansor, 2012). Pong, Lingxin and Erica (2005) from their research also found that there is strong correlation between academic achievement and authoritative parenting as compared to authoritarian and permissive parenting styles. Turner, Chandler and Heffer (2009), from their study with 264 college students indicated that both intrinsic motivation and self-efficacy determined academic performance and that authoritative parenting played a major role in the academic performance of college students. Results indicated that no relation was found for permissive and authoritarian parenting styles. The results of the study demonstrated that parental influence plays a significant role in young adults' academic performance. Authoritative characteristics such as warmth and supportiveness result in college student's increased intrinsic motivation. Although university students venture out on their own, previous experiences with their parents seem to continue to affect the students' success in college. Students who viewed that their parents encouraged their development of communication skills and autonomy while providing a set of boundaries to work within (i.e., authoritative parenting style) were predicted to have better academic success. These students not only tended to report higher GPAs, but also tended to have a higher academic self-efficacy.

Schunk (2008) discussed from his findings that the general motivation boosts are made when the parent allows the child to give an input in decisions, provide alternative choices and explanations, acknowledge the needs and feelings of the child, and state expectations in a clear manner. These general parental behaviours help accelerate intellectual development. It was also suggested authoritative behaviours such as giving the child hints or prompts helped encourage the child to be motivated to figure out problems by themselves by stimulating curiosity, opposed to supplying the child with the answer if struggled. Authoritative parenting practices provide guidance and limits while helping the child regulate themselves and take responsibility for their behaviours, which are lessons regarding academic discipline and many other skills. Although these are parenting techniques used when the student is just a child, the relationship built between the parent and child by this method follows them to college years and beyond.

Masud, Thurasamy and Ahmad (2014), in their research study conducted a systematic literature review of 39 studies and concluded that authoritative parenting style is instrumental in enhancing the academic performance of children. A characteristic of authoritative parenting, which is parental involvement, was studied by Paulson (1994) and the study revealed that parental involvement significantly predicted the academic achievement. The achievement outcome was found to be higher when parents involved themselves in children's academic activities. Another characteristic of authoritative parenting, that is, autonomy was studied in a longitudinal study by Wendy (1989) concluding that children's autonomous self-regulation, teacher-rated competency, adjustment, and school grades were completely associated with parental autonomy and support.

Parenting styles and academic performance have been studied primarily in children and adolescents. Baumrind (1991) found that children (ages 4-15 years old) of parents who were characterized as authoritative were the most motivated, the most competent, and the most achievement oriented. Strage and Brandt (1999) examined the role of parenting styles in the lives of college students and found that previous parenting behaviours continue to be important in the lives of college students as with children and adolescents. They found that the more autonomy, demand, and support parents provided, the more students were confident and persistent academically. Therefore, an authoritative parenting style emphasizing both responsiveness and demandingness appears superior in fostering higher academic performance (Reitman, Rhode, Hupp, & Altobello, 2002).

Another study tested high school students on their intrinsic motivation and the relationship it had to their perceived style of parenting. Based on the present study, authoritative parenting was positively related to intrinsic motivation, and several studies have linked intrinsic motivation with higher achievement outcomes (Riverse, 2008). A study conducted by Hoang (2007) in a self-reported survey, demonstrated that students who perceived their parents as authoritative had a higher tendency to adapt mastery goal orientation. This means the student had a higher desire to learn information or master a new skill with high abilities. More specifically for college aged students, maternal authoritativeness was significantly associated with a student's tendency to obtain mastery goals. Similarly, Boon (2007) too found students who reported their parents as authoritative had increased levels of self-efficacy and mastery goals.

The findings of Kriegbaum, Villarreal, Wu, and Heckhausen (2016) study suggested that shared agency with parents was consistently advantageous for college students' academic motivation. Shared agency, in this study, refers to the extent of which parents and students share the same academic goals and work together to obtain the goals. Kriegbaum et al. concluded that positive parental involvement and support is a noteworthy contributor to a college student's academic strives, goal, and pursuits. They shared that parents who were perceived to be more authoritative, had adolescents who tended to adopt goals that reflected intrinsic motivations, such as improving their abilities, the enjoyment of learning, and overcoming a challenge (Gonzalez & Wolters, 2009). Kriegbaum et al. (2016) also found that a non-shared agency among parents and children was correlated with a less beneficial motivational profile and academic achievement. College students who perceive higher parental directing have less motivation and more avoidance goal orientations. This demonstrates that parents and children who do not share similar academic goals result in decreased motivation. Authoritarian parents and their children would not share similar academic goals due to the high expectations that are displayed and the need to always do better.

Gonzalez and Wolters (2006) concluded from their study that students who viewed their parents as controlling, tended to report a greater focus in order to do better than their peers. Students who saw their parents as strict and dictating with a clear set of parent-defined rules tended to report a greater focus on doing their math work in order to outperform others (Gonzalez & Wolters, 2006).

Chen, Dong and Zhou (1997), conducted a research with 304 second-grade Chinese students and 512 parents in Beijing to examine the association between parenting styles and students' adjustment. They discovered that authoritarian parenting had positive relationship with students' aggressive behaviours and negative relationships with students' social competency and academic achievement. Authoritarian parents have high demands from their children, so children were found to have low self-perception and demonstrated lower academic achievement. The lowest cognitive competence and self-regulation was found in adolescents from neglectful families (Steinberg et al. 1994). Little or no communication skills and reserved behaviour in children were related to authoritarian practices (Baumrind 1971). Authoritarian parents tend to exert more rigid framework of rules and expect obedience from children as well, so self-regulation in children may be promoted but independence of self-expression is not allowed. Intrinsic motivation, self-reliance and perceptions of competence in adolescents are destabilized as a result of high demandingness, strict rules and obedience from the authoritarian parents (Steinberg et al. 1994). On the other end of the spectrum, children of permissive parents have freedom of expression and independence but due to the absence of a framework of rules they are emotionally less intelligent and have less social and intellectual competence as compared to others. Years later, Ang (2006), conducted a study with 548 Asian adolescents and found that authoritative fathers encourage adolescents' self-reliance in coping, problem-solving, and perseverance in academic challenges.

Zong, Zhang and Yao (2018), explored the relations between children's achievement goals, their view of different dimensions of parental involvement like home-based involvement, school involvement, and academic socialization. They further investigated the moderating role of parenting style, especially, parental autonomy support versus psychological control on the above mentioned factors. They observed positive association between home-based involvement and performance-approach goals, whereas, school related involvement was positively connected with mastery goals, and both these goals were positively linked to academic socialization. Gunderson, Donnellan, Robins and Trzesniewski (2018), concluded from their study that making parents aware of the positive effects of praise and the devastating effects of criticism might provide parents with more specific ideas about how to encourage their children to adopt goals and behaviours that sustain academic motivation. Another study by Leung and Shek (2018), with Chinese adolescents, in poor single-mother families examined the effects of family functioning and maternal expectations of adolescents' education on their achievement motivation. It was found that maternal expectations and family functioning positively predicted achievement motivation. Katerina, Alexopoulos and Katerina (2012), shared that authoritative parenting style results in intrinsic motivation among adolescents. Another study by Patrick, Leung and Kim (1998) revealed that authoritarian parenting predicts extrinsic motivation, authoritative parenting leads towards intrinsic motivation, and neglectful parenting results in no motivation.

A cross-sectional study by Murray (2012) on 8500 adolescents revealed that authoritative parenting was more effective as compared to that of authoritarian and permissive parenting style with regards to scores on measures of reading and math. Another study by Suet-ling, Jamie and Vivien (2010) on 20,000 adolescents' showed that authoritative parenting has positive relationship with school achievement while authoritarian parenting is negatively associated with school achievement. In particular, parents require to express realistic expectations for their children, so that the latter can find true goals for their studies (Leung, Lau, & Lam, 1998; Yahaya & Nordin, 2006).

Research findings from a study on 463 students from Hong Kong showed that parents of students from the highest academically focused schools rated themselves as greater in authoritativeness and as lower in authoritarian practices than parents of students from the lowermost academically oriented schools (Catherine & Lie, 1998). The use of structural equation modelling in a longitudinal study by Heaven and Joseph (2008) on 784 children revealed that adolescents with more authoritative parents experienced less of a decrease in conscientiousness than did students with less authoritative parents. A cross-sectional study by Dornbusch (1987) brought out that authoritative parenting leads towards higher grades as compared to authoritarian and permissive parenting which has lesser effect on the academic achievement leading towards low academic grades. Grade point average was found to be negatively related to the higher maternal beliefs on control dimension by a cross-sectional research study on 83 adolescents (Attaway & Bry, 2004).

A study by Kim and Rohner (2002) showed that authoritative and permissive parents were positive predictors of academic performance as compared to that of authoritarian parenting. Senk and Demir (2015) reported levels of higher self-esteem, lower depression, and better adjustment in students with authoritative parents compared to students with authoritarian parents. A study by Laurence (1992) brought out that stronger school engagement and positive school performance of students was observed amongst the students who ranked their parents as authoritative parents. Research on mothers and fathers parenting styles found that there is an additive effect in having two authoritative parents, which was associated with the most favourable outcomes in adolescents, and compensates when one parent has less effective parenting style (Simons & Conger, 2007). Similarly, McKinney and Renk (2008) mentioned that, seeing one parent as authoritative partly cushioned for emotional and adjustment problems in late adolescence

Bae (2015) suggested that children of authoritarian parents are more likely to compensate their independence in an unhealthy manner. They also reported that the college students of authoritarian parents felt that their parents do not believe they have the capability to be independent. Hence, this can lead to low academic motivation due to the perceived lack of confidence the parent displays in the child. Children of authoritarian parents are more likely to rebel due to the overwhelming sensation of never good enough or having any control. This may lead to lack of motivation in their academics and may experience fear to express a decision that is made by them which is opposed to their parents.

Gonzalez and Wolters (2009) studied permissive parenting and academic motivation. They suggested that permissive parents lead to a less adaptive pattern of motivation in children. They also suggested children who reported their parents as permissive were less concentrated on improving themselves or overcoming challenges while completing math homework. This was proposed to result from the lack of encouragement or example the parent displays by not engaging in learning new information or setting self-standards. Similarly, Hoang (2007) conducted a study which demonstrated that students who described their parents as permissive also reported to be less mastery goal oriented, which means the student had less desire to learn something new.

Wischerth, Mulvaney, Brackett, Perkins and Donna (2016) found that children of permissive parents had lower emotional intelligence and lower personal growth. It was explained that the possible lack of resulted personal growth in children of permissive parents may have derived from their inexperience with negative emotions due to the carelessness of the parents. Overcoming negative emotions such as fear, anger, or frustration positively helps the child's overall wellbeing, and can be related to their intrinsic motivation levels. If the parents do not put any pressure on the child to achieve, the child is not likely to have any motivation for themselves, especially if they have a low emotional intelligence or low personal growth level. Similar to the findings of negative personal growth, Barton and Hirsch (2015) concluded an overall lower score of wellbeing in the college students of permissive parents. Love and Thomas (2014) revealed from their study that permissive parenting predicted low levels of self-esteem and emotional well-being. Kenney, Lac, Hummer, Grimaldi, and LaBrie (2014) reported permissive parents as a predictor of poorer college adjustment compared to authoritative parenting. They said that low self-esteem and low emotional well-being leads to poor adjustment skills. Barton and Hirsch (2015) explained that students raised by permissive parents may have an unrealistic expectation in college due to their potential lack of standards or need to conform academically. This may lead to frustration and cognitive dissonance when challenged academically because it requires skills such as self-sufficiency and good self-regulation.

Exploring studies of neglectful parenting shows that adolescents who perceive neglectful parenting have lower overall mastery and self-efficacy, and high self-handicapping (Boon, 2007). Boon (2007) discussed that these issues are possibly caused by the lack of encouragement and support from parents as well as their lack of appropriate parental academic involvement. He explained many consequences, including risk of lower achievement and even school dropout. Parental uninvolvement was related to decrease in intrinsic and extrinsic motivation levels and less mastery approach goals (Kriegbaum et al., 2016). Hence, as neglectful parents neither control, demand, nor encourage, their children feel less drive to perform and exhibit lack of motivation.

Some research studies have clustered maternal and paternal parenting practices into joint parenting styles and studied how they are related to child development. Meteyer and Jenkins (2009), shared three parenting styles that were close to Baumrind's typology, namely supportive parents (like Baumrind's authoritative style), mixed–supportive parents (mother's parenting style is same as Baumrind's authoritative parenting style and father's style was close to Baumrind's authoritarian style) and non-supportive parents (similar to Baumrind's authoritarian parenting style). Another study by McKinney and Renk (2008), found out four joint parenting styles using sample of late adolescents in the age range of 18–22 years. The parenting styles found were - congruent authoritative (both parents adopting an authoritative parenting style), congruent authoritarian (i.e., both parents being authoritarian), combination of an authoritarian father–authoritative mother, and a permissive father–authoritarian mother group.

The study conducted by Lerdponkulrat, Koul and Sujivorakul (2012), reported that students who perceived their parents as empathetic, had higher learning orientations and students who perceived their parents as authoritarian had higher performance avoidance goals. The study by Gonzalez, Holbein and Quilter (2002) on 196 students found that authoritarian and permissive parenting styles were related to performance orientation, and that authoritative style was related to learning orientation. The study on 650 university students by Mahasneh (2014) reported positive relationships between learning and performance orientations and democratic parenting styles and that authoritative parenting style is the best predictor of achievement goal orientation. On the other hand, Gafoor and Kurukkan (2014), expressed that democratic parenting style is the most effective on achievement goal orientation.

The review of literature in the area of study habits showed that there have been various studies in this field, which relates study habits to academic success, motivation, emotional well-being, and effective parenting.

A study by John, Bulus and Tangsom (2020) with 199 secondary school students showed that there is strong positive significant correlation between study habits and academic performance of secondary school students. They shared that students with good study habits are more actively involved in the learning process and have found memory skills that work for them.

Shelke (2019), in her research found that effective learning depends on intelligence, intense and deep motivation, good physical health, stable home influences, fruitful guidance and instructions, emotional health of the learner, meaningful drills and repetition, concentration of effort, learning the whole, the meaningfulness of the situation, and its contact with the life of the learner. Narahari and Tewari (2015), in their study on adolescents from government Indian schools concluded that providing students with appropriate psychological counselling to inculcate better study habits has direct influence on academic performance. Yazdani and Godbole (2014), in their study concluded that study habits consisting of budgeting time, physical condition, reading ability, note taking, learning motivation, memory, taking examination and health, and achievement motivation have had significant relationship on academic performance and student with good study habits and high achievement motivation had better academic performance.

Butterweck (1957), in the book 'How to study', shares that students who succeed usually study on their own and follow a study technique that has been worked out by them and that incorporates desirable procedures. A successful student learns how to alternate work with rest, so that fatigue does not interfere with his/her successful achievement. The student has learned to read rapidly, take notes, attend carefully to classroom discussions, and in other ways to master the subject matter. The student has also discovered what good study habits are for him.

To understand these study habits and strategies further, Patel (1976) , from his study of study habits inventory, analysed and shared that study habits include: home environment and planning of work, reading and note taking habits, planning of subjects, habits of concentration, preparation for examination, general habits and attitudes, and school environment. Ley and Young (1998), through their research article shared that seeking assistance from peers and teachers, having high self-efficacy and effective time management skills, and being self-motivated are the characteristics of self-regulated learners. Another study by Jha and Kelleher (2006), asserted that even amongst students who have similar scholastic aptitude, some of them may perform better in terms of higher academic achievement when armed with better study habits and strategies. Sawar, Bashir, Khan, and Khan (2009) in their analysis on "Study Orientation of High and Low Academic Achievers at Secondary School Level" revealed that the high achievers had better study orientation and study attitude than the low achievers.

According to Menzel (1982), many students fail not because they lack ability but because they do not have adequate study skills. Students who have difficulty in college frequently do not have adequate study habits which ultimately affects their academic achievement. A study by Nagaraju (2004) also found that students usually do not devote sufficient time to their studies and seldom have proper study habits. Mendezabal (2013) from his study revealed that the participants did not have favourable study habits and attitudes. Among the noted unfavourable study habits were inefficient time management, lack of planning and concentration in their studies, poor skills in reading, ineffective test taking techniques, and failure to inform their teachers of their difficulties with school work and ask for their help. The participants also reported unfavourable attitudes toward teacher's classroom behaviour and methods. A study by Siahi and Maiyo (2015), was conducted with 85 students from grade 8 to 10. Results of the correlation indicated that there was significant positive relationship between study habits and academic achievement.

Nuthanap (2007) observed during his study that some students study more but they fail to achieve more. Others study less but achieve more. Success of each student definitely depends upon ability, intelligence and effort of students. Additionally, regular study habits too bring their own rewards in the sense of achievement of success. Misra (1992) conducted a study on assessing the level of test anxiety, self-concept, adjustment and study habits in predicting academic achievement; results indicated significant and positive correlation between study habits and academic achievement. Ramaswamy (1990) studied the relationship between study habits and academic achievement and found significant relationship between the study habits and academic performance variables. Mehta and Malhotra (1993) found study habits and study attitudes were the important predictors of academic achievement.

A study by Pathak (2020) with 100 adolescents revealed that there is a significant positive relationship between self-efficacy and study habits of adolescents. Students who had planned and studied well had the confidence to face their academics and eventually performed well. This lead to better self-efficacy (Lee & Lee, 2008). This study also revealed that there is a significant negative relationship between study habits and academic stress. They cited a study on achievement of rural girls which indicated that poor study habits were highly associated with higher stress. The results of this study indicated that self-efficacy beliefs are an important variable that contributes to the development of good study habits, better personality and high academic achievement. It showed that there is a positive relationship between study habits and academic self-efficacy, therefore the study suggested that it should be instilled in the minds of the young learners that if they have the confidence in their capabilities, they will surely manage the study related tasks well (Sharma, 2009).

According to a research to understand study skills further, it was found that effort, time, and environment regulation are among the study skills often connected to achievement (Burlison, Murphy & Dwyer, 2009; Lynch 2006). Pintrich (2004), explains that behaviour regulation is part of self-regulation, referring to individual attempts to control one's own behaviour. Important behaviour regulation activities in the academic environment or self-regulated study behaviour are effort regulation, time management, and environment management. Effort regulation refers to the ability to control the allocation and intensity of effort, with the goal of doing well in a course; time management involves activities such as making schedules for studying and allocating time for different activities; and environment management pertains to finding the optimal physical conditions for a learning environment, such as avoiding distractors like social media (Jacobsen & Forste, 2011) or people (Pintrich, 2004).

There is also a need to study underachievement and hence, Mandel and Marcus (1988) conducted a study on Psychology of underachievement, wherein, they presented that intelligence is merely one of the many factors that contribute to achievement. It is not about inability, but rather to do with incomplete utilization of one's potentials to the optimum levels despite complete ability. Underachievement is where the ability far exceeds the actual outcome, which is seen as achievement. They also concluded that faulty study habits and procrastination are the major reasons for underachievement. Hence, understanding achievement motivation is crucial for improving achievement. One theory of Achievement Motivation was proposed by Atkinson and Feather (1966), wherein they stated that a person's achievement oriented behaviour is based on three parts: the first part being the individual's predisposition to achievement, the second part being the probability of success, and third, the individual's perception of value of the task. Atkinson and Feather (1966) shared that the strength of motivation to complete any task is assumed to be a multiplicative function of the strength of the motive, the expectancy (subjective probability) that the act will have as a consequence that is the attainment of an incentive, and the value of the incentive: Motivation = f (Motive X Expectancy X Incentive).

One implication of expectancy X value-type of theory of motivation, is the notion that the anticipation of a negative consequence always produces negative motivation, that is, a tendency to inhibit activity that is expected to produce the negative consequence. If a student anticipates failure or a similar negative response, the student will actively try to avoid being in that situation. Similarly, if the student does end up confronted with a possible negative consequence, the student does little, if anything, to achieve a positive outcome. Alderman (1999), from his study adds that some individuals feel that success is based on ability, and failure is caused by a lack of ability. When competitive situations occur, many of these individuals often feel a need to protect themselves from failure or a perceived lack of ability, so they develop strategies such as withholding effort or setting unrealistic goals (too high or too low). Studies done by Tamsen and Livingston (1999), showed that students who value the outcome, put in more efforts and try more strategies to achieve the outcome. Similar studies done by Senecal, Koestner and Vallerand (1995) show that even when all possibilities of failure are removed from a situation, many students will procrastinate, quit, or not attempt the task if the outcome doesn't have any perceived value.

Motivation was found to be the best predictor of student achievement in the two studies which examined factors influencing student achievement and effects of the factors on students' achievement in learning the Japanese language through the medium of satellite television (Oxford, Park-Oh, Ito, & Sumrall, 1993; 1993). Fontana (1981) believed that satisfactory school learning is unlikely to take place in the absence of sufficient motivation to learn. In the study on predicting student success with the Learning and Study Strategies Inventory (LASSI), Hendrickson (1997) found that student's grade point average were best predicted by motivation and attitude. Hendrickson (1997) from his study found that motivation and attitude were the best predictors of student grade point average. The findings by Mahyuddin, Elias and Noordin (2009) showed that achievement motivation was significantly and positively correlated with academic achievement. Lirias, Maarten, Fraine, Damme, and Jan (2009) reported that achievement motivation was significantly and positively related to mathematics and language achievement. Diseth and Kobbeltvedt (2010) found in his studies that there was significant correlation between achievement motives, achievement goals, learning strategies and academic achievement.

Dupeyrat and Marine (2005) found that mastery goal orientation had a positive effect on learning actions and results, while performance goal orientation had a negative impact on learning activities and outcomes. They noted that mastery goal orientation through the mediation of effort expenditure had a positive effect on academic achievement. Additionally, Tanaka and Yamauchi (2000) also found that mastery goal orientation was positively associated with inherent interest and academic achievement, while performance goal orientation didn't had any significant influence on inherent interest or academic achievement. Shih (2005) from a study found that mastery approach orientation, performance-approach orientation and performance-avoidance orientation predicted distinctive patterns of learning. Riveiro, Cabanach and Arias (2001) revealed from their findings that only those students who reported a high mastery goal orientation exhibited more frequent use of cognitive and self-regulatory strategies. However, when multiple goals were taken into account, students who exhibited the most positive self-regulation were characterized as being influenced by both mastery approach and performance-approach goals.

Coleman (1993), in one of the study presented that high levels of achievement motivation are associated with striving for excellence and success without consideration of a particular reward. Studies conducted by Atkinson (1999) show that a percentage of students will work hard to achieve a task they do not enjoy, solely to maintain their high grade point average or high class rank. This tells us about student's attitude towards success. The students who have a high attitude of success, work hard to achieve success, regardless of the task. High achievement motivation and high achievement may be associated with normal perfectionism (Accordino, Accordino, & Slaney, 2000).

In a research study encompassing many field studies and laboratory experiments, Boggiano et.al (1992) revealed that achievement motivation positively influenced academic performance. It was found that motivational orientation predicted children's standardized achievement scores. Children with an intrinsic motivational orientation had higher reading and math scores and higher overall achievement scores compared to their extrinsic counterparts. Another study on academic intrinsic motivation, shows that it is positively and significantly related to students' achievement and perception of their academic competence, and inversely related to their academic anxiety (Gottfried, Fleming & Gottfried, 1994). Research by Lynch (2006) and Petersen, Louw and Dumont (2009), reported a positive relation between intrinsic motivation and adjustment. Baker and Siryk (1984) through their research showed that achievement motivation was correlated with academic adjustment. Moreover, Baker (2004) showed that lack of motivation is related to poorer adjustment to university.

Tella (2007) shared that highly motivated students performed better academically than low motivated students. Deci, Vansteenkiste, Simons, Lens, & Sheldon (2004) from his study also noted that engaging in learning behaviours with an intrinsic goal resulted in academic success and better test performance than engaging in behaviours with an extrinsic goal. A study on gender differences with regards to motivation concluded that females are highly motivated compared to their male counterparts (Sikhwari, 2014). A study by Sarangi (2015) with rural and urban students revealed that there was no significant difference with regards to achievement motivation between rural tribal – non tribal and rural boy – girl students. However, urban students showed high achievement motivation than the rural students.

Apart from these things, environment itself is also important, which is understood by McGregor's (2004) study, 'Space, power and classroom' that learning environment affects the engagement, motivation, self-esteem, attendance, well-being, and achievement of students. Emotional disturbance takes away the appetite to study and this can be seen from another study which shows that unhappiness at home and resentment towards the teacher also causes poor study habits in students (Ekeke & Telu, 2013).

According to Parker and Johnson (1981), an individuals' achievement motive may be seen as a personality trait. Each person has different degrees of achievement motivation. High achievers may be classified as driven, striving for success, competitive, or taking charge. Low achievers may be seen as quitters, non-participants, or failures. Each person approaches each situation with a unique combination of several achievement motives. These achievement motives are shaped by significant interactions in a child's early developmental years. They are learned motives, shaped by play, experience, and rewards or consequences for actions or behaviours. It is at this time when parents, role models, and teachers can have the greatest impact on the child's habits and values about achievement motivation. Hence, a study shows that social contexts (e.g., home environment) are characterized in terms of the degree to which they are autonomy supportive or "authoritative" versus controlling or "authoritarian," with research confirming that autonomy-supportive contexts enhance autonomous motivation whereas controlling contexts diminish autonomous motivation and enhance controlled motivation (e.g., Deci, Eghrari, Patrick, & Leone, 1994).

Interestingly, a study conducted by Bassett, Snyder, Rogers, and Collins (2013) which evaluated the concept of parenting styles on the instructor in a college classroom setting, had similar results. Bassett et al. concluded that teaching by the instructor who was perceived as authoritative by the students, had better correlation not only to the student's grades, but also to their interest in the subject matter. Students became more motivated by their increased interest in the class due to their instructors' authoritative teaching style, such as giving explanations for the rules, setting up expectations, offering guidance, and using appropriate communication methods. Although most commonly, parents are responsible for the motivation in students, nevertheless, this study demonstrates even other authority figures who can influence motivation in students. Similarly, Ricard and Pelletier (2016) found both parental support and teacher support as significant predictors for academic motivation in their study on high school students.

There were culture differences too observed concerning motivation levels. Bae (2015) found that although authoritative parenting was linked to higher motivation levels for students in the United States, it did not predict Japanese children's motivation levels in the same way. Japanese and other Asian cultured students identified their academic achievement motivation to be more influenced by factors other than parenting style, such as relationship with teachers, environment, and peer relationships.

Some studies enumerated that building up the right attitude to study among adolescents can be a product of parental activities, behaviour, thinking, personality, their interpersonal relationships, etc. Pajares (1996) found academic self-efficacy to be strongly associated with academic performance in college students, with positive correlations ranging from 0.49 to 0.71. Chemers, Hu and Garcia (2001).have also found that academic self-efficacy is a significant predictor of academic performance and expectations. Additionally, researchers have found that as students' academic expectations and self-efficacy increase, they are more likely to show higher academic performance (Chemers et.al.). Studies have shown that an authoritative parenting style in a parent-child relationship predicts a child's sense of mastery (i.e., belief in controlling one's environment) early in life (Turner & Johnson, 2003).

Research in the area of underachievement and home environment suggest that most often, the underachieving students are from families facing turmoil, stress, marital discord, job pressures, financial concerns, lack of emotional support, no leisure or family time and isolation from family (Turner & Johnson, 2003).

A small body of research has begun to investigate the socialization of coping in children and adolescents, which can be defined as, "parenting goals, practices, and styles that influence children's learning and utilization of emotional, cognitive, and behavioural strategies to manage personal and external demands that are perceived by either the parent or child to exceed the child's resources or capacities" (Miller, Kliewer, & Partch, 2010). Although there are a number of significant socializing agents in children's lives that contribute to the development of their coping styles (for example, peers, siblings, and teachers). However, the most extensive research, has focused on the role of parents, as the family is believed to be the earliest and most salient context by which, children acquire strategies to respond and adapt to stress (Bradley, 2007).

Kliewer, Sandler, and Wolchik (1994), proposed a conceptual model of coping socialization in which, parents are hypothesized to both indirectly and directly influence children's coping strategies through three pathways: (1) coaching, (2) modelling, and (3) the family context. It is noteworthy that conceptual models theorized on the development and socialization of other processes in childhood include similar pathways, such as emotional development (Eisenberg, Cumberland, & Spinrad, 1998), prosocial behaviour and empathy (Eisenberg, 1983), as well as emotion regulation (Calkins, 1994). The parallel pathways among these developmental frameworks provide further support that they are fundamental mechanisms by which, parents convey important messages to children and influence their behaviour.

Theoretical support for the role of coping coaching comes from research on both scaffolding and emotion coaching. Scaffolding is a process of structured learning that enables a child to progressively acquire new abilities just beyond their reach through support and instruction by their caregivers (Maccoby, 1992).

Tuzgol (1998), concluded from the research that parents exhibiting over-protective tendencies may cause their children to be unable to develop their own power, since they show increased level of control and sensitivity. Children brought up in this environment may show behaviours, such as being excessively independent from others, disappointed, insecure and rebellious. Additionally, these individuals cannot develop good emotional management skills and hence, may grow up to be individuals who are indecisive, discontented and irresponsible.

Finkenauer, Engels and Baumeister (2005), concluded from the data of 1,359 adolescents that the level of parental acceptance and control influenced children's social adjustment. Perceiving parents as authoritarian, those who restrict and exert high level of control, causes children to respond aggressively towards external factors. Hence, they encounter emotional problems such as stress and depression. In contrast, parents who are strict but also show support, acceptance and are involved in children's activities lead to more positive outcomes, which are reflected in their better psychosocial adjustment.

Neumeister (2004) from his research found that neurotic perfectionist children are more likely to have parents who are less encouraging, more demanding, and more critical. Perfectionists in this study described their parent(s) as setting high, non-negotiable standards as well as a low tolerance for showing emotions and lack of communication. Participants of this study reported their perfectionistic tendencies developed from the belief that they must meet the high expectations and the fear of disappointing others. In order to prove it to their parents, such students aim for perfection and believe they can always do better. This can significantly alter one's academic motivation, however, these tendencies can cause health issues such as anxiety or sleep deprivation.

According to Cummings, Davies and Campbell (2000), parental support is indicated by involvement, acceptance, emotional availability, being warm, and responsive. Support has been associated with positive outcomes, such as the prevention of substance use and deviant behaviour (Barnes & Farrell, 1992), depression and antisocial behaviour (Bean, Barber & Crane, 2006), and externalizing problem behaviour (Shaw, Keenan & Vondra, 1994). An adequate amount of behavioural control has been thought to influence child development positively, whereas insufficient (poor parental monitoring) or excessive behavioural control (like, parental physical punishment) has been usually related to negative child outcomes, such as deviancy, delinquency, depression, and anxiety (Galambos, Barker & Almeida, 2003). Parental behavioural control has to do with controlling the child's behaviour, whereas, parental psychological control refers to an intrusive type of control in which parents try to manipulate children's thoughts and emotions (Barber, Stolz, Olsen, Collins & Burchinal, 2005). As the psychological control has manipulative and intrusive nature, it has been linked with negative child developmental outcomes resulting in depression, delinquent behaviour, and relational regression (Kuppens, Laurent, Heyvaert & Onghena, 2013).

Some previous research has been conducted on the associations between parenting styles and parent-adolescent conflict intensity and frequency. Conflict intensity is the level of emotional arousal that occurs during conflict, while, conflict frequency means how often conflict occurs. Smetana (1995), found that association of parenting styles' with conflict frequency and intensity were very similar across different parenting styles. In contrast, Assadi, Smetana, Shahmansouri and Mohammadi (2011), reported that frequency was higher for authoritarian parents and lower for parents who were authoritative, but only authoritative parenting was related to intensity.

A study on parenting styles shows that permissive and authoritarian parenting styles are correlated with negative psychological and behavioural outcomes (Driscoll, Russell, & Crockett, 2008). Maximum studies with

Western samples indicate that authoritative parenting is associated with higher levels of parent–adolescent cohesion (Nelson, Walker, Christensen, Evans & Carroll, 2011) and less conflict frequency, conflict intensity, and overall conflict (Smetana, 1995; McKinney & Renk, 2011). In contrast, an authoritarian parenting results in less cohesion (McKinney & Renk, 2011) and high conflict frequency, intensity and entire conflict (Smetana, 1995; McKinney & Renk, 2011). Similarly, Sorkhabi and Middaugh (2013), investigated data from American adolescents with varied ethnic backgrounds and found that adolescents having authoritative parents recounted less conflict than those having authoritarian parents. Fuligni (1998), analysed and concluded from the research study that adolescents of both Asian, American, and European American cultures felt that it was more essential to discuss and share their problems with their parents. Another study by Barnhart, Raval, Jansari, & Raval, (2013) found that Indian college students in comparison to US college students thought that permissive parenting was more effective and helpful.

A related study by Gray and Steinberg (1999) reported that autonomy granting parenting has a wide spectrum of healthier child outcomes such as academic achievement, psychological wellbeing, and a healthy socially adaptive behaviour. Parental autonomy was also found to lead to better adjustment and higher levels of psychosocial functioning (Deci & Ryan, 2000). Authoritarian parents were too strict and supervised their children more than necessary, whereas indulgent and neglectful parents could not provide sufficient monitoring and guidance. Adolescents having non-authoritative parents desire more behavioural autonomy, which then doesn't get fulfilled in an appropriate way (Bush & Peterson, 2013). A similar study found that authoritative parents have children and adolescents who approve the validity of parental authority (Trinkner, Cohn, Rebellon, & Gundy, 2012; Darling, Cumsille & Alampay, 2005). Authoritarian parents have too rigid rules, whereas, indulgent and neglectful parents define rules too leniently (Baumrind, 2005). Hence, adolescents and parents may not recognize opportunities to debate and negotiate appropriate boundaries, which then can make youth to question the validity of parental authority. Research study by Bhattacharyya and Pradhan (2015) showed that adolescents' use of preventive and instrumental coping strategy is related to perception of parental demandingness.

Research has found that children of emotion coaching parents are better able to manage emotions and have fewer adjustment problems (Stocker, Richmond, & Rhoades, 2007). According to a study by Rivers (2006), which is in accordance with findings of Baumrind, children raised with the democratic parenting style have a strong belief in their self-capability when they face any difficulties. Thus, it can be said that democratic parenting style contributes to one's self-efficacy. Although, the democratic parenting style has many positive outcomes in general, there are some studies that emphasize the positive effects of the authoritarian parenting style. Rivers (2006), shared that children of authoritarian parents also have beliefs of self-competence when they face academic tasks and difficulties.

Zimmer-Gembeck and Locke (2007), found that the combination of parental involvement, structure, and autonomy support was positively associated with active coping at both home and school and negatively related to wishful thinking and avoidant coping at home. Silk, Shaw, Skuban, Oland, and Kovacs (2006) from their research reported that children of depressed mothers used less effective strategies, including focusing their attention on the desired item or passively waiting for the task to end, while children of non-depressed mothers engaged in more adaptive strategies, including using active distraction (for example, singing or dancing around the room). Research by Langrock, Compas, Keller, Merchant, and Copeland, (2002) and Jaser et.al. (2005) has also shown that as stress in the family context rises, children and adolescents of depressed parents use less adaptive coping strategies indicating that in stressful situations where individuals require the most effective coping strategies, they increasingly use more maladaptive approaches.

In a large-scale study involving 1,990 children and adolescents with age ranging from 7-16 years old, Eschenbeck, Kohlmann, and Lohaus (2007), found that girls favoured emotion-focused coping while boys favoured avoidant coping. Interestingly, gender differences were more obvious in coping with social situation than academic challenges. A study by Kaufmann et al. (2000) revealed that adolescents whose parents had characteristics of authoritative parents adopted self-enhancing attributions and strategies having low levels of failure expectations. Another study on attribution and parenting style showed that adolescents who did not see their parents as authoritative were more likely to relate achievement outcomes to external reasons or to low ability (Glasgow, Dornbusch, Troyer, Steinberg, & Ritter, 1997).

Recent evidence by Compas et al., (2011) has been reported regarding the effects of a family group cognitive behavioural preventive intervention program designed to teach children to use more adaptive coping strategies to deal with the stress associated with parental depression (that is, secondary control coping) as well as to teach parents to use more positive parenting practices (for example, warmth, structure) in interactions with their children. Children in the intervention group reported significantly fewer internalizing problems through the 12-month follow-up and had significantly fewer diagnoses of depression and any other DSM disorder at the 24-month follow-up compared to the children in the information only comparison condition. Further, we reported that, the intervention led to significant changes in children's secondary control coping strategies as well as positive parenting practices, which both partially mediated the effects of the intervention on children's emotional and behavioural adjustment. The design of the study provided an optimal opportunity to examine how the intervention might have facilitated changes in parenting behaviours that uniquely contributed to changes in children's coping strategies as well as how changes in children's coping strategies might have uniquely contributed to changes in parenting behaviours.

This present study will further explore the effects of three parenting styles namely, authoritarian, permissive and authoritative parenting styles and children's' study habits, achievement motivation and their use of coping strategies.

Hypotheses

I. There will be significant difference in the study habits and achievement motivation of children between authoritarian, authoritative and permissive parenting styles.

II. The children of authoritative parenting style will have better study habits as compared to children of permissive parenting style.

III. The children of authoritative parenting style will have better study habits as compared to children of authoritarian parenting style.

IV. The children of authoritarian parenting style will have better study habits as compared to children of permissive parenting style.

V. The children of authoritative parenting style will have high motivation as compared to children of permissive parenting style.

VI. The children of authoritative parenting style will have high motivation as compared to children of authoritarian parenting style.

VII. There will be no significant difference in motivation between children of authoritarian and permissive parenting style.

VIII. There will be significant difference in the coping strategies (positive reappraisal, problem solving, cognitive avoidance and acceptance or resignation) of children between authoritarian, authoritative and permissive parenting styles.

IX. The children of authoritative parenting style will be better at positive reappraisal coping strategy as compared to children of authoritarian and permissive parenting style.

X. The children of authoritative parenting style will be better at problem solving coping strategy as compared to children of authoritarian and permissive parenting style.

XI. The children of authoritarian parenting style will use cognitive avoidance coping strategy more often as compared to children of permissive and authoritative parenting style.

XII. The children of authoritarian parenting style will use acceptance and resignation coping strategy more often as compared to children of permissive and authoritative parenting style.

XIII. There will be significant positive correlation between study habits and motivation.

CHAPTER- III
METHOD

Method

Participants

The participants of the present study consisted of 580 adolescent boys and girls. They were in the age range of 13 to 14 years. The students were from grade 8 and 9 from English medium schools in Mumbai. The sample comprised of boys and girls of different educational boards (SSC, ICSE and CBSE). Initially 626 participants were screened for the study, out of which 580 were selected who completed the questionnaires suitably. The most common form of nonprobability sampling; convenient sampling was used, as it involves choosing participants primarily on the basis of their availability and willingness to respond (Shaughnessy, Zechmeister, & Zechmeister, 2009).

The students were asked to respond through questionnaires about their study habits, achievement motivation and the strategies that they use to cope with stress. Additionally, they were inquired regarding perception of their parents parenting style through a questionnaire. Additionally, 5% of the parents were also interviewed to validate the responses provided by the adolescents. The variables of study habits, motivation and coping with stress could get affected by exams. Hence, good precautions were taken while collecting data and they were not tested during, immediately before or after the exams.

Inclusion criteria

- English medium students were part of the study
- Schools from Mumbai were included in the study

Exclusion criteria

- Students from other boards like IGCSE & IB were not part of this study
- Special schools were excluded from the study

Tools

The study was conducted by using one demographic questionnaire, one interview schedule and four psychological tools:

i. Demographic questionnaire – A questionnaire was prepared to collect demographic information like name, age, gender, date, school details and educational board. The questionnaire also included statements about requirement of participants consent with a brief introduction of the researcher and the research to be conducted. It also included statement of acknowledgement from parents wherein their signature was requested and were asked to mark Yes/No depending on their decision of participation in the study.

ii. Test of Study Habits & Attitudes (TSHA):

In the present study, study habits were measured by using Study Habit Inventory developed by Mathur (2002). This test is created for use with school, college and university students, ranging from age 13+ years to adulthood. It is intended to measure the study habits and attitudes of students. The test is appropriate for use with both genders. It discriminates between good and poor study techniques of students, and is expected to be helpful to teachers and counsellors. In this inventory, the study habits have been considered to be constituted of nine different kinds of study behaviours. These are: Attitude towards teachers, Home environment, Attitude towards Education, Study habits, Mental conflict, Concentration, Home assignment, Self-confidence and Examination (Mathur, 2002). There are 60 items seeking responses in the categories of 'Yes', 'Doubtful' and 'No'. An example of the item is 'I do not keep attention seeking things like Radio, TV, Film Magazines, Novels, Toys, etc. in my room.' The scoring is stencil type wherein only the correct responses are to be counted, those which are visible through the stencil.

The reliability of the inventory on the basis of test-retest method was +0.87 for age group of 13 to 16 and +0.89 for age group of 16 and above. The validity was established through criterion validity with other tests. The reliability coefficients with Survey of Study Habits & Attitudes in English – by Mathur, Survey of Study Habits & Attitudes (General) by Purohit and Academic Achievement Scores were found to be +0.63, +0.77 and +0.65 respectively.

iii. Achievement Motivation (n-Ach) Scale (AMS):

In the current study, achievement motivation was measured using achievement motivation scale by Deo and Mohan (2011). The questionnaire is available in Hindi and English version. In the present study, the English version was used which consisted of 50 items. The achievement motivation was distributed into academic motivation, need for achievement, academic challenge, achievement anxiety, importance of grades, meaningfulness of task, relevance of school/college to future goals, attitude towards education, work methods, attitude towards teachers, interpersonal relations, individual concern, general interests, dramatics and sports (Deo & Mohan, 2011). Out of 50 items, 13 are negative and 37 are positive items. One such item is 'I set standards for myself and then strive to achieve them.' The questionnaire is of the self-rating type and can be administered in a group with 5 points to rate i.e. always, frequently, sometimes, rarely, never. It has no time limit. The scoring device is simple stencil type having a numerical weightage from 4 to 0 for positive in the above order of rating scale and the reverse of it for the negative items.

The scale has test-retest reliability of 0.69 and split-half reliability of 0.56 and item validity of 0.54. The reliability coefficients were found to be 0.69 and 0.78 for male and female groups respectively. Cronbach's alpha coefficient for overall male and female was found to be 0.86.

The validity was found through concurrent validity and the coefficient of correlation with the projective test of Achievement motivation was observed to be 0.54. Additionally, the scaled scores were also correlated with the Aberdeen Academic motivation inventory of Entwistle (1968) which yielded a correlation coefficient of 0.75.

iv. Coping Responses Inventory – Youth (CRI):

In this study, coping strategies were measured by using Coping responses inventory developed by Moos (1993). It is a 48 item self-report inventory designed for age group of 12 to 18. It assesses the cognitive and behavioural responses an individual uses to cope with a recent problem or stressful events. Participants were asked to describe, in short, a recent stressful incident and the items were based on the incident. CRI can be easily hand-scored in about 5 minutes by using the scoring template printed on the carbonless sheet of the answer sheet.

The inventory consists of 8 specific coping strategies people use which are: Logical Analysis, Positive Reappraisal, Seeking Guidance and Support, Problem Solving, Cognitive Avoidance, Acceptance and Resignation, Seeking Alternative Rewards and Emotional Discharge (Moos, 1993). Chronbach's alpha has been the most frequently reported coefficient of reliability which range from 0.71 to 0.94. The validity of the CSI has been assessed in number of ways like – Factor structure, construct validity and criterion validity. This test was purchased from Psychological Assessment Resources, Inc (PAR).

v. Parental Authority Questionnaire (PAQ):

Parenting style was measured by using parental authority questionnaire developed by Buri (1991). It measures perceived parenting style which means that the questionnaire assesses parental authority or disciplinary practices from the perspective of the child (Buri, 1991). Hence, it is administered to a child. This questionnaire provides us with three parenting styles, namely permissive, authoritative and authoritarian parenting style. The tool consists of 30 items; 10 items for each parenting style. Each student have to answer it on a five point rating scale of 1= strongly disagree to 5= strongly agree. It can be scored manually by adding up the ratings provided for each question of 3 parenting styles. Highest score denotes that particular style to be the dominant style. Buri reported Cronbach coefficient alpha values for the subscales ranging from 0.87 to 0. 74. The content, criterion and discriminant validity were also reported to be high.

vi. Interview:

Parent Interview Schedule was prepared and it consisted of 12 questions. The responses were to be marked in 2 options of Yes and No. The questions were designed to gain information about their child's study habits and motivation. Interview of parents was conducted as a qualitative tool to support the data obtained from quantitative tools on students study habits and achievement motivation.

Variables

In the current study, one Independent variable and three dependent variables were assessed, which are as follows:

Independent Variable

1. Parenting Styles – Parenting style was measured at three levels.

- Authoritarian
- Permissive
- Authoritative

Dependent Variables

1. Study Habits

2. Achievement motivation

3. Coping with stress

Operational definition of variables

1) Parenting styles–It refers to a psychological construct demonstrating standard strategies that parents use in their child rearing (Buri, 1989). In the current study, we have measured three parenting styles which are as follows:

i. Permissive parenting style –In this style, parents tend to make fewer demands of their children, allowing them to regulate their own activities as much as possible. The parents are not firm and relatively very rare in giving punishments.

ii. Authoritarian parenting style – They are very directive towards their children and expect unquestioning obedience from their children. They are detached and show less warmth towards their children.

iii. Authoritative parenting style – They are characterized as providing clear and firm directions, but this disciplinary clarity is moderated by warmth, reasoning, flexibility and negotiation.

2) Study habits – In the present research, the study habits have been assessed as nine major areas of the study techniques, habits and attitudes which are: Attitude towards teachers, Home environment, Attitudes

towards Education, Study habits, Mental conflict, Concentration, Home assignment, Self-confidence and Examination (Mathur, 2002).

3) Achievement motivation – The current study defines achievement motivation in terms of academic motivation, need for achievement, academic challenge, achievement anxiety, importance of grades, meaningfulness of task, relevance of school/college to future goals, attitude towards education, work methods, attitude towards teachers, interpersonal relations, individual concern, general interests, dramatics and sports (Deo & Mohan, 2011).

4) Coping with stress - In the present study, coping with stress is defined as coping responses for stressful life circumstances in eight different ways. These responses are – Logical Analysis (LA), Positive Reappraisal (PR), Seeking Guidance and Support (SG), Problem Solving (PS), Cognitive Avoidance (CA), Acceptance and Resignation (AR), Seeking Alternative Rewards (SR) and Emotional Discharge (ED) (Moos, 1993). The details of each are provided as follows –

Approach coping responses

- Logical Analysis – It is one's cognitive attempts to understand and prepare mentally for a stressor and its consequences.
- Positive Reappraisal – In this strategy, one makes cognitive attempts to construe and restructure a problem in a positive way while still accepting the reality of the situation.
- Seeking Guidance and Support – These are behavioural attempts to seek information, guidance or support.

- Problem Solving – Here, the person makes behavioural attempts to take action to deal directly with the problem.

Avoidance coping responses

- Cognitive Avoidance – It is the person's cognitive attempts to avoid thinking realistically about a problem.

- Acceptance or Resignation – In this strategy, one makes cognitive attempts to react to the problem by accepting it.

- Seeking Alternative Rewards – These are behavioural attempts to get involved in substitute activities and create new sources of satisfaction.

- Emotional Discharge – Here, the person makes behavioural attempts to reduce tension by expressing negative feelings.

5. Adolescent – In this study, children or adolescents are defined as students studying in class 8th and 9th, who are in the age range of 13 to 14 years.

Research Design

In the present study, between group design and correlation analysis was used. There is one Independent variable at three levels and three Dependent variables in this study. Qualitative method at data collection level was used for 5 % of the parent sample to verify the responses obtained from questionnaires completed by students.

Procedure

In this study, data was collected from school students. Hence, contacting school for the data collection was the first step. Data was collected from different schools of Mumbai, catering to three different educational boards. The three different educational boards were SSC, ICSE and CBSE.

The procedure commenced with seeking permission from schools by scheduling an appointment with the Principals. The Principals were informed regarding the nature of the study, time required and ethical considerations of this research study. After seeking the relevant permission, participants were selected between the age range of 13-14 years studying in grade 8th and 9th.

Before initiating the study, a letter of consent was sent across to the parents stating the nature of the study and the ethical considerations involved in the same. Thereafter, as per the convenience and availability of the students in their respective schools, the survey was conducted over a few months. Instructions were given to the participants regarding filling up of questionnaires. The questions were explained, if the student failed to comprehend the meaning of the questions. After completion of the questionnaires, the participants were debriefed about the study. The debriefing included the instruction that, during the process of survey if anyone experienced any overwhelming or negative emotions/ thoughts, then they should approach the school counsellor. While collecting the data, no student shared any uncomfortable feeling with the researcher.

A total of 612 sets of questionnaires were collected. Thirty two sets were excluded from the study due to incomplete responses or missing of one/two questionnaires, leaving a total of 580 sets for analyses.

Additionally, 5 % of the parents of students participating in the study, that is, 35 parents were interviewed by using a pre-defined Interview Schedule to check the data obtained from study habits and achievement motivation questionnaires. The parents to be invited for interview were selected based on their availability and readiness to participate in the interview. Each parent was met individually for approximately 10 minutes. Subsequently, based on their responses, student study habits and motivation were grouped into poor, moderate or good study habits and motivation. The same was compared with the scores of Test of study habits & attitudes, and Achievement motivation scale.

Statistical Analysis

One-way analysis of variance (ANOVA) and Product moment correlation was used to analyse the hypotheses. Post Hoc test was conducted to analyse the mean differences if ANOVA was found to be significant.

Ethical Consideration

The participants of the study were minor students aged 13 and 14 year olds. Hence, consent was sought from parents. The form included sufficient information in order for them to make an informed decision with regards to participation. In addition, the consent form clearly explained the elements of parental consent, risk of harm, and confidentiality involved and the precautionary measures adopted for the same. The confidentiality of the information provided by research subjects and the anonymity of respondents has been maintained. Each participant's response was assigned a code and hereafter all the scoring and data entry was according to these codes. An individual participant could withdraw from the study at any point of time. The participants were chosen from different educational boards so that the results could be generalized to a larger population. There was no apparent risk or harm to any research subjects during the course of the study.

CHAPTER- IV
RESULTS

RESULTS

Parents play a pivotal role in the development of their children. They should be aware and conscious of their parenting practices as they are being constantly observed by their children to learn to deal with emotions and behave appropriately. Hence, role modelling as a part of parenting, can help establish appropriate structure leading to good study habits and intrinsic motivation as well as can show demonstration of effective coping strategies. Parenting style is defined as a group of parents' attitudes and behaviours towards their children and an emotional atmosphere in which the parents' behaviours are conveyed (Darling & Steinberg, 1993).

In the present study, the findings were analysed by using One-way ANOVA. As the sample size varied for each level of Independent variable, Levene's statistic was carried out to test the equality of each comparison group as required for performing ANOVA. The data was scanned for the presence of outliers and were removed from the data while calculating the statistical value. Post hoc tests were applied when the F value was found to be significant. Tukey's HSD (Honestly Significant Difference) was used to identify which particular differences between pairs of means were significant. Additionally, the findings of the Parents Interview schedule were matched with the scores obtained from study habits & achievement motivation questionnaires. These findings demonstrated that reported study habits and motivation by adolescents matched with parents' perception of their children's study habits & achievement motivation.

The present research aimed to study the impact of parenting styles on study habits, achievement motivation, and coping with stress amongst adolescents. In the present study, 580 adolescents were surveyed and the classification of number of parents in each perceived parenting style is presented in Figure 1 and the number of boys and girls studied in the present study is demonstrated in Figure 2.

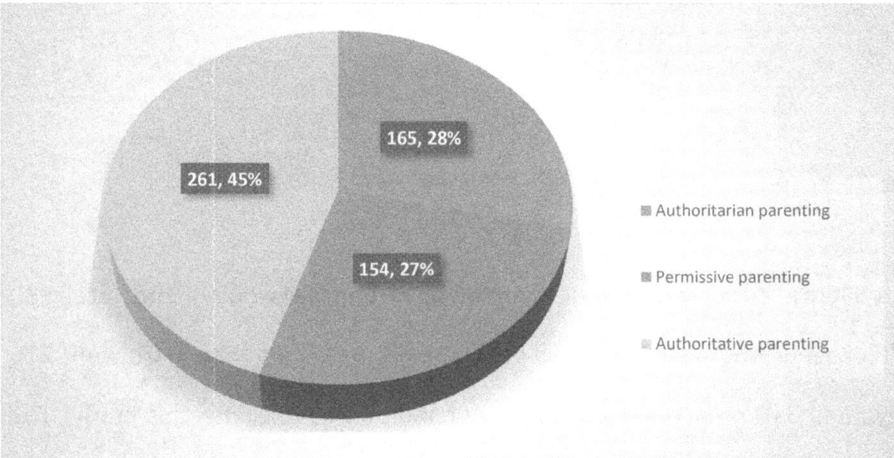

Figure 1. Percentage of Three Parenting Styles Being Used by the Parents

Figure 1 illustrates the percentage of parents using each parenting style among the total of 580 parents who were studied. Highest among the three parenting styles was the Authoritative parenting style. 45% parents preferred using it making it the highest used style. The pie chart shows that 261 out of 580 parents were authoritative. Next in the line was the authoritarian parenting style. 28% parents, that is, 165 out of 580 parents used this style. Lastly, permissive parenting style was seen to be the least preferred style with 27% of parents using it. Permissive parenting style was used by 154 out of 580 parents in this study.

Figure 2. Number of Adolescent Boys and girls in this Study

Figure 2 displays the number of boys and girls out of the total 580 adolescents who were surveyed in this study. It shows that there were 270 boys and 310 girls who were given questionnaires to fill for this study. The difference in the count of boys and girls is because of more girls giving consent and willingly participating in the study.

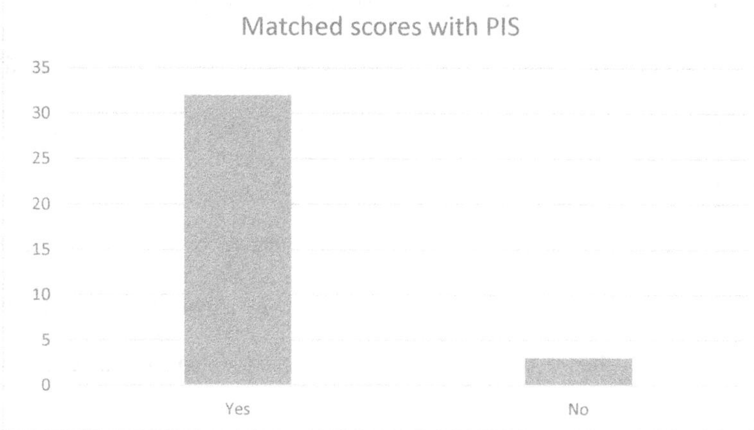

Figure 3. Matched scores of Parent Interview Schedule with adolescents scores of study habits and achievement motivation

In this research study, 5 % of parents that is 35 out of 580 parents were interviewed. These parents were selected and interviewed on the basis of convenient sampling, that is, depending on their availability. The data was used to check the reported study habits and motivation as provided by adolescents. The interview questions tried to gain data about adolescents with regards to their time management, distraction and motivation towards studying. Figure 3 demonstrates the results of these Parent interviews. It was found that 32 out of 35 students who reported about their study habits and motivation matched with the data from Parent Interview Schedule (PIS), which shows that 91 % of adolescents reported correctly regarding their study habits and motivation.

The first hypothesis stated that, "there will be significant difference in the study habits and achievement motivation of children between authoritarian, authoritative and permissive parenting styles; for testing this hypothesis one-way analysis of variance was conducted and the results of the same were significant, thereby supporting the first hypothesis. The results of the same are shown below factor wise.

The first factor investigated was study habits with respect to different parenting styles. One- way analysis of variance was conducted to test this hypothesis. The results of the descriptive statistics of means and standard deviations for study habits are shown in Table 1, whereas, Table 2 presents the output of one way analysis of variance for study habits and Table 3 depicts the Tukeys HSD post hoc analysis.

Table 1

Descriptive Statistics for Study Habits

Parenting style	*N*	*Mean*	*Std.Deviation*
Authoritarian	165	30.98	7.89
Permissive	154	27.86	6.69
Authoritative	262	36.76	6.97

The results of the descriptive statistics of the means and standard deviations are shown in Table 1. It indicates that the adolescents study habit is effective in authoritative parenting style (M = 36.76), as compared to authoritarian parenting style, (M = 30.98) and permissive parenting style (M = 27.86). However, the significant mean differences can be found out by employing one-way ANOVA.

Table 2

One-way ANOVA of Study Habits for Different Parenting Styles

Source of Variation	*SS*	*Df*	*MS*	*F*	*P-value*
Between Groups	8412.81	2	4206.41	81.76	0.00
Within Groups	29738.41	578	51.45		
Total	38151.22	580			

Table 3

Post Hoc Analysis for Study Habits of Different Parenting Styles

Treatment pairs	*Mean difference*	*Significance*
Authoritarian & Permissive	3.12	0.01
Authoritarian & Authoritative	5.78	0.01
Permissive & Authoritative	8.89	0.01

* The mean difference is significant at the 0.01 level.

The output for the one-way ANOVA procedure to compare the means of the three parenting styles on the study habits are shown in Table 2. There was a statistically significant difference between groups as determined by one-way ANOVA, $F(2, 578) = 81.76$, $p = .00$. The results from the one-way ANOVA do not indicate which of the three groups differ from one another, so, it is of interest to follow the analysis with a post hoc test. Thus, in this study to compare pairs of means, post-hoc Tukey's HSD was performed, which shows all three mean differences to be significant. These significant mean differences indicate that the adolescents study habits is best developed in authoritative parenting style, followed by authoritarian parenting style and least developed in permissive parenting style.

The second hypothesis stated that 'the children of authoritative parenting style will have better study habits as compared to the children of permissive parenting style'. This hypothesis has been fully supported by the ANOVA and post hoc analysis.

The third hypothesis states that 'the children of authoritative parenting style will have better study habits as compared to the children of authoritarian parenting style' has also been supported as the mean difference is significant according to post hoc analysis.

The fourth hypothesis also stands accepted suggesting that children of authoritarian parenting style have better study habits as compared to children of permissive parenting style.

The second factor under study was achievement motivation related to the three parenting styles. For testing this hypothesis, one-way analysis of variance was performed. The results of the descriptive statistics of means and standard deviations for achievement motivation are shown in Table 4, whereas, Table 5 provides the output of one way analysis of variance for achievement motivation and Table 6, shows the Tukey's HSD post hoc analysis.

Table 4

Descriptive Statistics for Achievement Motivation

Parenting Style	*N*	*Mean*	*Std. Deviation*
Authoritarian	165	128.66	18.24
Permissive	153	125.36	14.18
Authoritative	262	141.18	16.66

The results of the descriptive statistics of the means and standard deviations are shown in the Table 4. It indicates that the adolescents achievement motivation is higher in authoritative parenting style (M = 141.18), as compared to authoritarian parenting style, (M = 128.66) and permissive parenting style (M = 125.36). However, the significant mean differences can be found out by calculating one-way ANOVA.

Table 5

One-way ANOVA of Achievement Motivation for Different Parenting Styles

Source of Variation	*SS*	*Df*	*MS*	*F*	*P-value*
Between Groups	29507.37	2	14753.68	54.06	0.00
Within Groups	157739.2	578	272.91		
Total	187246.6	580			

Table 6

Post Hoc Analysis for Achievement Motivation of Different Parenting Styles

Treatment pairs	*Mean difference*	*Significance*
Authoritarian & Permissive	3.29	NS
Authoritarian & Authoritative	12.52	0.01
Permissive & Authoritative	15.82	0.01

* The mean difference is significant at the 0.01 level.

The output of one-way ANOVA procedure to compare the means of the three parenting styles on the achievement motivation of their children are shown in Table 5. There was a statistically significant difference between groups as determined by one-way ANOVA, $F(2, 578) = 54.06$, $p = .00$. The results from the one-way ANOVA do not indicate which of the three groups differ from one another, hence a post hoc test needs to be conducted. Thus, in this study to compare pairs of means, post-hoc Tukey's HSD was calculated, which showed two mean differences to be significant. These mean differences indicate that the adolescents' achievement motivation is positively influenced by authoritative parenting style as compared to authoritarian and permissive parenting styles.

The fifth hypothesis suggested that the children of authoritative parenting style will have high motivation as compared to children of permissive parenting style has been significantly supported as the mean difference is significant according to post hoc analysis.

The sixth hypothesis also stands accepted supporting that the children of authoritative parenting style will have high motivation as compared to the children of authoritarian parenting style according to one-way ANOVA and post hoc values.

The seventh hypothesis stated no significant difference in achievement motivation between the children of authoritarian and permissive parenting style was also supported by the data as the post hoc analysis showed no significant mean difference between the two groups.

The third factor under study was coping with stress related to different parenting styles. The eighth hypothesis stated 'that there will be significant difference in the coping strategies (positive reappraisal, problem solving, cognitive avoidance and acceptance or resignation) of children between authoritarian, authoritative and permissive parenting styles. This hypothesis was tested by applying one-way ANOVA and the results of the same were significant, thereby supporting this hypothesis. Four one-way ANOVA's were conducted to test this hypothesis, which was further subdivided into four more hypotheses.

The ninth hypothesis of the study stated that 'the children of authoritative parenting style will be better at positive reappraisal coping strategy as compared to children of authoritarian and permissive parenting style'; for testing this hypothesis, a one-way analysis of variance was conducted. The results of descriptive statistics of means and standard deviations for positive reappraisal coping strategy are shown in Table 7, whereas, Table 8 provides the output of one way analysis of variance of this coping strategy and Table 9 depicts the Tukey's HSD post hoc analysis.

Table 7

Descriptive Statistics for Positive Reappraisal Coping Strategy

Parenting Style	*N*	*Mean*	*Std.Deviation*
Authoritarian	165	7.21	2.94
Permissive	153	6.86	2.72
Authoritative	262	9.79	2.68

The results of the descriptive statistics of the means and standard deviations are shown in the Table 7. It indicates that the positive reappraisal coping strategy is more used by adolescents with parents using authoritative parenting style (M = 9.79), as compared to authoritarian parenting style, (M = 7.21) and permissive parenting style (M = 6.86). However, the significant mean differences can be found out by calculating one-way ANOVA.

Table 8

One-way ANOVA of Positive Reappraisal Coping Strategy for Different Parenting Styles

Source of Variation	*SS*	*Df*	*MS*	*F*	*P-value*
Between Groups	1106.85	2	553.42	72.3	0.00
Within Groups	4424.15	578	7.65		

Total	5530.99	580

Table 9

Post Hoc Analysis for Positive Reappraisal Coping Strategy

Treatment pairs	*Mean difference*	*Significance*
Authoritarian & Permissive	0.35	NS
Authoritarian & Authoritative	2.59	0.01
Permissive & Authoritative	2.94	0.01

*. The mean difference is significant at the 0.01 level.

The output of one-way ANOVA procedure to compare the means of three parenting styles on the adolescent's use of positive reappraisal coping strategy are shown in Table 8. There was a statistically significant difference between groups as determined by one-way ANOVA, $F(2, 578) = 72.3$, $p = .00$. The results from the one-way ANOVA do not indicate which of the three groups differ from one another, so, the analysis needs to be followed up with a post hoc test. Thus, in this study to compare pairs of means, Post hoc Tukey's HSD was performed. As shown in Table 9, the Tukey post-hoc test revealed that the use of positive reappraisal coping strategy in the authoritative parenting styles differed significantly from authoritarian and permissive parenting style ($p < .01$). This Tukey post hoc test indicates that the authoritative parenting style leads to a higher use of positive reappraisal coping strategy in adolescents. Thus, hypothesis 9 is accepted.

The tenth hypothesis of the study stated that 'the children of authoritative parenting style will be better at problem solving coping strategy as compared to the children of authoritarian and permissive parenting style'. This hypothesis was tested by one-way analysis of variance. The results of descriptive statistics of means and standard deviations for problem solving coping strategy are shown in Table 10, whereas, Table 11 shows the output of one-way analysis of variance of this coping strategy and Table 12 provides the Tukey's HSD post hoc analysis.

Table 10

Descriptive Statistics for Problem Solving Coping Strategy

Parenting Style	***N***	***Mean***	***Std. Deviation***
Authoritarian	165	6.99	2.76
Permissive	153	7.29	3.08
Authoritative	262	10.26	3.12

The results of the descriptive statistics of the means and standard deviations are shown in the Table 10. It indicates that adolescent's use of problem solving coping strategy is higher in authoritative parenting style (M = 10.26), as compared to authoritarian parenting style, (M = 6.99) and permissive parenting style (M = 7.29). However, the significant mean differences can be found out by employing one-way ANOVA.

Table 11

One-way ANOVA of Problem Solving Coping Strategy for Different Parenting Styles

Source of Variation	*SS*	*Df*	*MS*	*F*	*P-value*
Between Groups	1408.56	2	704.29	77.67	0.00
Within Groups	5241.18	578	9.07		
Total	6649.75	580			

Table 12

Post Hoc Analysis for Problem Solving Coping Strategy

Treatment pairs	*Mean difference*	*Significance*
Authoritarian & Permissive	0.30	NS
Authoritarian & Authoritative	3.26	0.01
Permissive & Authoritative	2.96	0.01

*. The mean difference is significant at the 0.01 level.

The output of the one-way ANOVA procedure to compare the means of the three parenting styles on the adolescent's use of problem solving coping strategy are shown in Table 11. There was a statistically significant difference between groups as determined by one-way ANOVA, $F(2, 578) = 77.66$, $p = .00$. The results from the one-way ANOVA do not indicate which of the three groups differ from one another, so, it is of interest to follow the analysis with a post hoc test. Thus, in this study to compare pairs of means, post hoc Tukey's HSD was performed. As shown in Table 12, the Tukey post-hoc test revealed that the scores of problem solving coping strategy in the authoritative parenting style differed significantly from authoritarian and permissive parenting style ($p < .01$). Thus, Tukey post hoc test indicates that the authoritative parenting style group is statistically and significantly higher on developing problem solving coping strategy in adolescents than the authoritarian and permissive parenting style groups. Thus, hypothesis 10 is supported.

The 11th hypothesis of the study stated that 'the children of authoritarian parenting style will use cognitive avoidance coping strategy more often as compared to children of permissive and authoritative parenting style.' For testing this hypothesis a one way analysis of variance was used. The results of descriptive statistics of means and standard deviations for cognitive avoidance coping strategy are shown in Table 13, whereas, Table 14 presents the output of one way analysis of variance of this coping strategy and Table 15 depicts the Tukey's HSD post hoc analysis.

Table 13

Descriptive Statistics for Cognitive Avoidance Coping Strategy

Parenting Style	***N***	***Mean***	***Std. Deviation***
Authoritarian	165	10.11	3.05
Permissive	153	8.41	3.36

Authoritative	262	7.16	2.98

The results of the descriptive statistics of the means and standard deviations are shown in the Table 13. It indicates that the adolescent's use of cognitive avoidance coping strategy is higher in authoritarian parenting style (M = 10.11), as compared to permissive parenting style (M = 8.41) and authoritative parenting style (M = 7.16). However, the significant mean differences can be found out by calculating one-way ANOVA.

Table 14

One-way ANOVA of Cognitive Avoidance Coping Strategy for Different Parenting Styles

Source of Variation	*SS*	*Df*	*MS*	*F*	*P-value*
Between Groups	881.15	2	440.57	45.78	0.00
Within Groups	5563.07	578	9.62		
Total	6444.21	580			

Table 15

Post Hoc Analysis for Cognitive Avoidance Coping Strategy

Treatment pairs	*Mean difference*	*Significance*
Authoritarian & Permissive	1.69	0.01
Authoritarian & Authoritative	2.95	0.01
Permissive & Authoritative	1.25	0.01

* The mean difference is significant at the 0.01 level.

The output of one-way ANOVA procedure to compare the means of the three parenting styles on the adolescent's use of cognitive avoidance coping strategy are shown in Table 14. There was a statistically significant difference between groups as determined by one-way ANOVA, $F(2, 578) = 45.78$, $p = .00$. The results from the one-way ANOVA do not indicate which of the three groups differ from one another, so, it is needed to be followed up with a post hoc test. Thus, in this study to compare pairs of means, Post hoc Tukey's HSD was performed. As shown in Table 15, the Tukey's post hoc test revealed that the scores of cognitive avoidance coping strategy in the authoritarian parenting style differed significantly from authoritative and permissive parenting style ($p < .01$). This Tukey's post hoc test indicates that the children of authoritarian parenting style are statistically and significantly higher on use of cognitive avoidance coping strategy than children of authoritative and permissive parenting style groups. Thus, the eleventh hypothesis is accepted.

The 12th hypothesis of this study stated that 'the children of authoritarian parenting style will use acceptance and resignation coping strategy more often as compared to children of permissive and authoritative parenting style.' For testing this hypothesis, a one-way analysis of variance was conducted. The results of descriptive statistics of means and standard deviations for acceptance and resignation coping strategy are shown in Table 16, whereas, Table 17 presents the output of one way analysis of variance of this coping strategy and Table 18 depicts the Tukey's HSD post hoc analysis.

Table 16

Descriptive Statistics for Acceptance and Resignation Coping Strategy

Parenting Style	*N*	*Mean*	*Std. Deviation*
Authoritarian	165	8.78	3.29
Permissive	153	7.92	3.24
Authoritative	262	6.47	2.82

The results of the descriptive statistics of the means and standard deviations are shown in the Table 16. It indicates that the adolescent's use of acceptance and resignation coping strategy is higher in authoritarian parenting style (M = 8.78), as compared to permissive parenting style (M = 7.92) and authoritative parenting style (M = 6.47). However, the significant mean differences can be found out by employing one-way ANOVA.

Table 17

One-way ANOVA of Acceptance and Resignation Coping Strategy for Different Parenting Styles

Source of Variation	*SS*	*Df*	*MS*	*F*	*P-value*

Between Groups	575.64	2	287.82	30.5	0.00
Within Groups	5453.58	578	9.44		
Total	6029.22	580			

Table 18

Post Hoc Analysis for Acceptance and Resignation Coping Strategy

Treatment pairs	***Mean difference***	***Significance***
Authoritarian & Permissive	0.87	NS
Authoritarian & Authoritative	2.31	0.01
Permissive & Authoritative	1.44	0.01

The output for one-way ANOVA procedure to compare the means of the three parenting styles on the children's acceptance and resignation coping strategy are shown in Table 17. There was a statistically significant difference between groups as determined by one-way ANOVA, $F(2, 339) = 8.02$, $p = .00$. The results from the one-way ANOVA do not indicate which of the three groups differ from one another, so, it is of interest to follow the analysis with a post hoc test. Thus, in this study to compare pairs of means, post hoc Tukey's HSD was performed. As shown in Table 18, the Tukey's post hoc test revealed no significant difference between the authoritarian and permissive parenting styles, however authoritative parenting style differed significantly from the other two parenting styles.

Thus, the 12th hypothesis is partially supported. The results show that the adolescents of both authoritarian and permissive parenting styles use acceptance and resignation coping strategy more often as compared to authoritative parenting style.

Table 19

Correlation between Study Habits and Achievement Motivation

Variables	***Study habits***	***Achievement motivation***
Study habits	1	0.64
Achievement motivation	0.64	1

The result of Pearson product moment correlation between the study habits and the achievement motivation as shown in Table 19 is r (578) = 0.64, p<.01, which shows significant correlation between the two factors. Hence, the 13th hypothesis which states that there will be significant positive correlation between the study habits and the achievement motivation has been supported by the current study.

CHAPTER- V
DISCUSSION

Discussion

Parenting is an important area of research as several studies show that family climate plays a major role in all areas of development of an adolescent, be it social, emotional or cognitive (Karavasilis, Doyle & Markiewicz., 2003; Kauffman et al., 2000; Maccoby & Martin, 1983).

Parents being role models, play a vital role in their child's overall development. Family environment is hence one of the factors influencing children's cognitive, emotional, social, and behavioural competence (Nancy & Laurance, 1993). Many theories highlight that parenting plays a significant role in child development, which has driven researchers to investigate the influence of parenting on child development.

Moitra and Mukherjee (2012), point out that home is the place where a normal and healthy development of any child starts, and family becomes the backbone of an individual. From this perspective, family is considered to be the basic ecology to establish a child's behaviour by positive or negative reinforcement. Variations in parenting styles and parent–child relationship qualities are long-standing research topics in developmental and family psychology. Previous research has shown that parenting styles are critical family context factors, which are closely related to parent–adolescent relationships (Shek, 2002). Children need to experience a healthy and positive psycho-social development, which enables them to succeed in every field of life, including education.

The present study intended to examine the influence of different perceived parenting styles on study habits, achievement motivation, and coping with stress among adolescents. Overall, based on our results, it can be seen that authoritative parenting style comes across as better than authoritarian and permissive parenting styles with regards to development of necessary study habits, achievement motivation, and appropriate coping strategies among adolescents. The variable of study habits, which was studied by applying one way ANOVA, showed that adolescents had better study habits when their parents had authoritative parenting style, followed by authoritarian parenting style. Children of Permissive parents showed the least developed study habits according to our analysis. Second one way ANOVA was conducted for the factor of achievement motivation among students in different parenting style groups. The results clearly showed that adolescents with authoritative parents had better scores on achievement motivation as compared to authoritarian and permissive parenting. The results also showed no difference in achievement motivation of adolescents between authoritarian and permissive parenting styles. The third factor, of coping with stress, was studied using One way ANOVA's and the results pointed out that authoritative parenting is most effective in developing appropriate approach coping strategies of positive reappraisal and problem solving when compared with authoritarian and permissive parenting styles. The results of one way ANOVA for the coping strategy of cognitive avoidance, which is an avoidance coping strategy, was seen to be used more frequently by adolescents with authoritarian parenting style, followed by permissive parenting style. It was seen to be least used by the adolescents with authoritative parents according to the data findings. The coping strategy of acceptance and Resignation, which is also an avoidance coping strategy, was also examined by applying one way ANOVA and the results showed that authoritarian parenting lead to higher use of this strategy among adolescents as compared to permissive and authoritative parenting styles.

The results from Parent Interview Schedule was matched with the adolescents' scores from study habits and achievement motivation questionnaires. It showed that 91 % of adolescents reported correctly about their study habits and achievement. This was done to support the quantitative data obtained from the adolescents.

The first factor of study habits, which shows that authoritative parents help build better study habits among their children because they are both demanding and responsive compared to authoritarian and permissive parenting styles. Being demanding helps establish necessary structure and goal for the children, while responsiveness helps by making parents accessible and available for their children to negotiate and discuss.

Results are consistent with the study of Yahaya and Nordin (2006), which was conducted with 216 secondary school students to understand the relationship between the academic self-concept, motivation, and parenting styles with achievement. Pearson-r and the Multiple Regression technique were used to conclude the relationship between the factors. The results showed that the authoritative style out of the four parenting styles, had the highest value with motivation, achievement, and academic self-concept. They further described that building up the right attitude to study among adolescents can be a product of parental activities, behaviour, thinking, personality and their interpersonal relationships. As a result, child rearing pattern of parents may be an important factor in achieving good study habits. Parents specifically need to express the realistic expectations for their children, so that children can find true goals for themselves.

A study carried out by Narahari and Tewari (2015), entailed a total of 290 participants, wherein a survey was conducted regarding parenting and academic achievement. An independent samples *t*-test was conducted to compare the college GPA of students that have high authoritative parents and students that have low authoritative parents. This study suggested that students with high authoritative parents had moderately greater likelihood to attain high college GPAs than students with other types of parents.

Additionally, a study by Kumar (2014), was conducted with 240 college students to understand the effect of parenting styles on adolescent problems. Results of ANOVA indicated that both non-caring and caring, that is, pampering or overprotection are detrimental for the children which can lead to various problems like physical and health fitness issues, self and self-image, family, educational, vocational, economic, friendship, and sex problems. Rejection of a child from parents proved to be the worst as it produces an extremely high level of mental strain. So, it was recommended that the adolescents' problems could be overcome by moderately caring parents and understanding the needs and attitudes of children by their parents and teachers.

Sarwar (2016), used the case study approach and collected data through in-depth interviews of mothers of adolescents. The researcher used coding method of data analysis. Words such as beating, anger, and cursing were placed in the authoritarian style category, whereas words such as understand, ask, and discuss showed the authoritative parenting style. On the other hand, words like lenient, say nothing, and neglect was seen as an indication of the permissive parenting style. The study examined the influence of parenting style on children's behaviour and concluded that authoritarian parenting leads to delinquent behaviour and low academic achievement. According to their study, good parenting is authoritative in which parents keep their eyes on their children and try to understand the mind-set of their children. This prevents delinquency and leads to better academic achievement. The research further suggested many reasons for positive outcome of this parenting. The authoritative parents present themselves as role models and demonstrate same behaviours as they want from their children. Children may learn to internalize these behaviours. Fixed rules and discipline may educate the children about their responsibilities. Authoritative parents display emotional understanding and exhibit adequate control, as a result, children might learn to understand others' emotions and also learn to manage their own sentiments. Our findings are consistent with this study and provides us with important insights into the reasons for authoritative parenting being a positive influence for study habits of children.

Turner, Chandler and Heffer (2009), from their study with college students stated that authoritative parenting is an effective predictor of academic performance. They mentioned several characteristics of the authoritative approach that are helpful in positive academic outcomes. Authoritative parenting styles support the autonomy of children, which helps in better academic performance and provide children with appropriate direction.

A study by Chowdhury and Ghose (2014), with 620 students from class VII to II year students of college indicated that there is a strong relationship between sagacious parenting, which is authoritative parenting and good study habits. They reasoned that realistic expectations of parents from their children as well as parents' own principles and actions in their daily lives were responsible in inculcating good study habits in their children.

Ekeke, and Telu (2013), from their study with 200 students investigated some practical steps that parents take to improve their child's study habits and recommended that, good parents provide their children with advantages that they actually need for their school, career, and that helps children to develop proper aims and goals for future life. They further stated that these parents draw up a time table for their children and encourage them to follow through, devote their time to teach their children, are responsive to their child's education by providing learning facilities as well as conducive and motivating learning atmosphere at home. These characteristics are part of authoritative parenting style and thus our results are in sync with this study. In our study, authoritative parents have shown to be positively influencing the study habits of their children.

There are many correlational studies, which have also shown a positive correlation between academic achievement and authoritative parenting (Pong, Johnston & Chen, 2010; Roche, Ensminger, & Cherlin, 2007). A correlational study was conducted by Yasmin, Kiani and Chaudry (2014), on 350 college students, wherein, correlation between parenting styles and academic performance was computed through Pearson's correlation coefficient (r). The results of study showed that the authoritative parenting style of mother and father had a positive relationship with academic performance. Another study showed that the authoritarian and permissive parenting style of mother and father were negatively correlated with academic performance. They stated the characteristics of authoritative parenting style, that is, warmth, supervision & psychological autonomy granting to be reasons for positive association with the grades achieved at school level (Nyarko, 2011).

However, a study by Masud et.al, (2019), with 456 school students of grades 8, 9 and 10 brought out different results. This study investigated the determinants of academic performance by stressing on the role of parents in adolescent students A regression analysis was carried out and the results showed that the affectionless control group, which according to our study is authoritarian parenting style group, was the only parenting style found to be independently improving academic performance. A cross-sectional survey from Iran with 400 high school students also provides support for the authoritarian parenting style to be influencing the academic performance positively (Rahimpour, Moghadam, Moghadam & Hashemian, 2015). They reasoned that authoritarian parenting style makes children obedient and proficient as they demand and establish strict rules. Their children have better study habits as they have high expectations. This study is consistent with our hypothesis of authoritarian parents leading to better study habits as compared to permissive parents.

Another study was conducted by Masafoor (2013), with 262 high school students to study the connection between different parenting styles and students' educational achievement. Analysis of the results using regression and ANOVA revealed that there is a meaningful positive relationship between authoritarian parenting style and educational achievement. Also, the calculations indicate that there is a negative association between educational achievement and autocratic (authoritative) parenting style. There is no association noted between permissive parenting style and academic achievement. The explanation offered was that parents' authority demonstrated in the authoritarian parenting in the form of structure and following of rules can bring out a range of cognitive and social results like better educational achievement, better adaptability, less behavioural problems and higher level of competence.

A review of 39 studies published by Masud, Thurasamy and Ahmad (2014), assessed the effect of parenting styles on academic performance. The review very pertinently described how the authoritative parenting style was the dominant and most effective style in terms of determining academic performance in the West and European countries while Asian cultures show more promising results for academic success with the authoritarian parenting style.

A study was conducted by Rani (2013), on 100 secondary school students to find out the relationship between study habits and home environment of the students studying in secondary school of Haryana. The coefficient of correlation of study habits with home environment components of control, protectiveness, punishment, conformity, social isolation, reward, deprivation of privileges, nurturance, and permissiveness were not found to be significant. Hence, the study showed no relationship between home environment and study habits of children.

Leung, Lau and Lam (1998), after their cross-sectional study on 382 adolescents from grade 10 and 11 of schools in Hong Kong, United States, and Australia concluded that academic achievement was negatively associated with academic authoritarianism, but displayed no connection with academic authoritativeness. According to them, academic authoritativeness showed no relation with academic achievement because when children receive good grades, the reinforcement from self-esteem enhancement and from peers and teachers may overwhelm the effect of parental reinforcement. On the other hand, when children receive poor grades, parental support and help may not be sufficient, and may need to be coupled with effective learning strategies.

A survey in San Fransisco with 7836 adolescents, Dornbusch, Ritter, Leiderman, Roberts and Fraleigh (1987), found that Asian American parents were more authoritarian than European American parents. These findings then suggest that Asian Americans should have poorer academic results than European Americans, however, paradoxically Asian Americans generally show better academic results. Dornbusch et.al (1987), enumerated that for Asian Americans, parental influence on school performance is not as important as peer influence, and the negative effects of authoritarian parents are outweighed by positive peer influence.

One study conducted by Barnhart, Raval, Ashwin, and Raval (2013), with 226 college students in India and 517 college students from the United States highlighted that permissive parenting is effective compared to those of authoritarian and authoritative parents. Their explanation of these unexpected findings was that Indian college students considered permissive parenting as more helpful and effective and selected this as a style they would employ in the future more than US students and this may be related to processes of globalization. Patel, Amin and Power (2002), found that with India moving towards increasing modernization has brought about attitude change in parenting, including more individualistic values. The advances in technology, has given increased access to Western media and culture emphasizing more permissiveness and autonomy granting in parenting. These messages communicated via the media definitely influence the perceptions of effective parenting among younger generation, like the college students of this study. Such effect may indicate greater surrendering of parental control and greater than before autonomy granting. Thus, a new troop of parents and their college aged children may characterize changing notions of parenting compared to older generations.

Therefore, there are studies, which show positive relationship between Authoritative parenting style and study habits or academic performance. Some studies also show negative relationship or find other parenting styles to be more effective than authoritative parenting style. However, the results from the current study clearly state that authoritative parenting style is best for optimum development of study habits followed by authoritarian parenting style. Permissive parenting style has been found to be the least effective style in developing appropriate study habits among adolescents.

The results of the second variable of achievement motivation clearly showed that adolescents with authoritative parents had better scores on achievement motivation as compared to authoritarian and permissive parenting. No difference was seen in achievement motivation of adolescents between authoritarian and permissive parenting styles. This shows that children of parents providing proper guidance are better achievers. Most of the students perceived that when their parents provided clear and firm direction, set up rules, and are flexible to adapt to their needs, then they can respect them and follow most of the rules clearly (Elias & Yee, 2009).

These results are supported by the findings of a study conducted by Mohan, Kaur and Kaur (2013), with 100 adolescents in the age range of

14-17 years to understand the effect of parental attitude (acceptance or rejection) on achievement motivation and self-concept of adolescents. The results were analysed by using ANOVA, which shows that adolescents in the Parental acceptance group had better level of achievement motivation as compared to those in the parental rejection group. They reasoned that parental acceptance leads to formation of positive emotions and attitudes in children and this leads to better achievement motivation (Xitao & Michael, 2001). When there is acceptance by the parents, the home environment is congenial and such parents are likely to be effective role models. Thus, children learn more appropriate behaviour from such effective role models (Rim & Scheictewr, 2002). Thus, in our study parental acceptance group is similar to authoritative parenting group which has shown to influence achievement motivation positively.

A study by Hoang (2007), to examine motivational outcomes, as predicted by parenting practices with 140 students in the age range of 14-17 years used multivariate analysis and multiple regression to analyse the findings. The results showed that parents who are perceived to be more authoritative, have children with the tendency to adopt a mastery goal orientation. That is, they adopt goals that reflect their enjoyment of learning and for the inherent sake of learning. The findings further indicated a negative relation between students reporting permissive parents and a self-reported adoption of mastery orientation. Specifically, students reporting permissive parents also reported being less mastery oriented. It was discussed that perhaps the lack of guidance, that often characterizes a permissive parent, does not encourage the inherent interest in mastering new information and developing self-set standards for achievement that often defines mastery oriented students. This finding is similar to that of Baumrind (1967), where she observed the children of more permissive parents as being less independent and self-reliant.

Tang, Li, Sandoval and Liu (2018), carried out a study with 226 Chinese 10th grade students and one respective parent (147 fathers and 165 mothers) to investigate the relation between parenting styles and students' academic motivation. Path analysis showed that the mothers' authoritative parenting was positively related to intrinsic motivation. They described that a family atmosphere where mothers show warmth and support, as well as demonstrate and monitor clear standards for children's conduct and success, thereby facilitate children's autonomy and competence. Hence, children are more likely to complete academic tasks for its own sake and understand the significance of learning for their future success. Children experience volition when they receive effective feedback and clear direction from their mothers, further leading to academic success. It was also found that permissive parenting style was positively related to an external regulation that is extrinsic motivation. Permissive parenting is characterized as less demanding. Children may feel absence of clear structure, rules, and regulations leading to motivation only in presence of external rewards. Permissive parenting was considered to be harmful for child development because it failed to give a sense of competence (Milevsky et al., 2007). This is consistent with our findings, which shows that authoritative parenting style is seen to be effective in improving achievement motivation in adolescents as compared to authoritarian and permissive parenting styles.

A research study by Gota (2012), was conducted on a sample of 2116 (763 females and 1353 males) undergraduate first year students to examine the impact of parenting styles, academic self-efficacy, and achievement motivation on academic achievement. The results of regression analysis showed that an authoritative parenting style had a significant and positive indirect effect on achievement motivation via its significant and positive effect on academic self-efficacy. That is, students who characterized their parents as authoritative had higher academic self-efficacy than their counterparts who rated their parents as non-authoritative, and in turn these students had higher achievement motivation. They shared that students who are more intrinsically motivated are from families that display more involvement, higher levels of nurturance and encouragement of more autonomy (that is, the characteristics of authoritative parents), whereas parental psychological control (that is, the characteristic of authoritarian parents) was associated with controlled motivation (Turner, Chandler, & Heffer, 2009). They further referred to a research by Maccoby and Martin (1983), which mentioned that authoritative parents are characterized by high levels of nurturance & involvement, reasoning, setting clear standards, enforcing rules firmly, encouraging autonomy, and providing open communication. Therefore, a significant and positive direct effect of authoritative parenting style on the academic self-efficacy and significant and positive direct and indirect effects on the achievement motivation of students can be seen.

A study by Kosterelioglu (2018), was carried out on 497 students and their parents who were selected via a simple cluster sampling to determine the effects of parenting styles, as perceived by parents, on high school students' achievement goal orientations. Results of multiple regression analysis showed that democratic parenting styles were found to have the strongest and the most significant impact on learning approach orientation, whereas, overprotective and permissive parenting styles had the most significant impact on learning avoidance orientation. Analysis also showed that authoritarian and overprotective parenting styles had the most significant impact on performance orientations. Furthermore, they stated that children raised with the democratic parenting style have a strong belief in their self-capability when they face academic tasks and difficulties, and hence they move towards learning approach orientation. From this perspective, it can be said that democratic parenting style contributes to one's self-efficacy (Rivers, 2006).

Another study on 650 university students by Mahasneh (2014), reported positive relationships between learning and performance orientations and these factors were also studied in relation with democratic, authoritarian and permissive parenting styles. Authoritative parenting style was found to be the best predictor of achievement goal orientation.

A study was conducted by Llorca, Richaud, and Malonda (2017), with 100 undergraduate students to examine the correlation between undergraduate student's academic motivation and perceived parenting style. The results from bivariate correlation demonstrated that authoritative parenting style and academic motivation levels were statistically significant.

A study by Arenliu, Hoxha, Berxulli and Gashi (2014), with 610 high school students investigated the association of specific maternal parenting styles with motivation. The results specified significant positive correlation between authoritative parenting style scores with intrinsic motivation orientation. Other two types of parenting showed no significant correlation with intrinsic motivation. They shared that children who grow up with authoritative parents show a high level of involvement in academic tasks and activities, and higher intrinsic motivation. Authoritative parents encourage their children to be independent and self-confident, by creating an environment that demonstrates expectations and encourages communication. The enthusiasm that parents show in their children's education helps to create an environment of encouragement and self–motivation, with an emphasis on intrinsic motivation (Creekmore, 2010).

However, the results from the multivariate analyses of a study by Hoang (2007), with 140 students in the age range of 14-17 years indicated authoritarian parenting as a positive predictor of a performance approach orientation. This means that students reporting authoritarian parents also reported a greater desire to achieve high level of performance. They further stated that if the rules of the household indicate that only an A grade is acceptable, a student may focus on doing whatever possible to accomplish that grade, regardless of mastery of information, which reflects external motivation. Multivariate analyses also revealed a positive relation between permissive parenting and students reporting themselves as more performance approach oriented. One explanation for this finding offered by the study was that the laissez-faire parenting style may leave students no choice but to adhere to the normative standards, which are sometimes imposed by the school because of the lack of standards imposed by the parents. Adhering to normative standards imposed by schools, may not always be as maladaptive if the standards are positive, functional, and lead to progress toward a broader goal.

A study by Tang *et.al.* (2018), with 226 Chinese adolescents showed that the mothers' authoritarian parenting style was negatively related to external regulation, that is an extrinsic motivation. They reasoned that in Chinese culture, control and strictness inherently reflect that parents authentically care, love, as well as govern their children with the hope to foster their optimal development, both academically and socially. This type of control is in fact perceived as supportive instead of restrictive.

There are studies which continue to prove that authoritative parenting leads to better motivation in children. There are also few studies, which show authoritarian or permissive parenting to be better predictors of motivation in children. However, the results of this study clearly show that authoritative parenting style leads to better achievement motivation in their children as compared to the other two parenting styles. Hence, the benefits of authoritative parenting resulting in better motivation adds evidence to the universal importance of supportive parenting for optimal development of achievement motivation among children across cultures.

The results of the third variable, coping with stress, pointed out that authoritative parenting style is the most effective in developing appropriate approach coping strategies of positive reappraisal and problem solving when compared with authoritarian and permissive parenting styles. The coping strategy of cognitive avoidance, which is an avoidance coping strategy was seen to be used more frequently by adolescents with authoritarian parenting style, followed by permissive parenting style; and least used by adolescents of authoritative parenting style. Acceptance and resignation coping strategy, which is also an avoidance coping strategy, was found to be used more by children of authoritarian parents as compared to permissive and authoritative parenting styles.

A study by Bhattacharyya and Pradhan (2015), was conducted to investigate the effect of perceived paternal parenting styles on coping strategies of adolescents. A sample of 180 adolescents was collected from grade 10th and 11th. The results of the analysis of variance and hierarchical multiple regression analysis showed that adolescents' perception of paternal responsiveness was found to significantly predict strategic coping in adolescents. Responsiveness is a characteristic of authoritative parenting style and hence the results are in sync with our findings. They further shared that autonomy granting parenting has a wide spectrum of healthier child outcomes like academic achievement, psychological wellbeing, and health socially adaptive behaviour (Gray & Steinberg, 1999). Parental autonomy is also found to lead to better adjustment and higher levels of psychosocial functioning (Deci & Ryan, 2000).

Mohan, Kaur and Kaur (2013), concluded from their study that self-concept of adolescents with parental acceptance was high as compared to other parents. The study was conducted on 100 adolescents in the age range of 14-17 years. Results of ANOVA showed that self-concept of adolescents with parental acceptance was high as compared to parental rejection group. They discussed that parents who accept their children, communicate their expectations clearly, express concern for their children, monitor them tend to raise competent children with less involvement in problem behaviours and better adjustment (Strage, 1998). Parental rejection, on the other hand, leads to aggression in children and aggressive children often show maladjusted behaviours (Moffitt, 1993). Thus, parental acceptance enables children to be better in emotional regulation and have a better sense of self confidence, self-esteem, and overall positive self-concept. This is in line with our findings of authoritative parenting, which is like parental acceptance group, which leads to approach coping strategies.

A research by Finkenauer, Engels and Baumeister (2005), concluded from their data of 1,359 adolescents that, the level of parental acceptance and control influenced children's social adjustment. Results of multiple regression analyses showed that perceiving parents as authoritarian, those who restrict and exert high level of control causes more children to respond aggressively towards external factors. Hence, they encounter emotional problems such as stress and depression. In contrast, parents who are strict but also show support, acceptance and are involved in children's activities lead to more positive outcomes, better self-esteem, which is reflected in their better psychosocial adjustment. They illustrated that adolescents who grow up in supportive, nurturing families where parents are emotionally involved, responsive to their children's needs, and interested in their children's lives are less likely to develop problem behaviours than adolescents who grow up in distant, conflictive families where parents are uninvolved, neglectful, or rejecting (Lamborn, Mounts, Steinberg & Dornbusch, 1991).

The study of Zimmer-Gembeck and Locke (2007), with 487 adolescents was carried out to find associations between adolescents' relationships with families and teachers, and coping behaviours. They found that adolescents with more positive family relationships used more active coping with problems at home and school. They further shared that the combination of parental involvement, structure, and autonomy support was positively associated with active coping at both home and school, and negatively related to wishful thinking and avoidant coping at home.

A study by Kuppens and Ceulemans (2019), with 600 families was conducted to find clusters of joint parenting styles, and its effect on children. Results of ANOVA indicated that children with two authoritarian parents displayed the poorest behavioural outcomes. These children showed increased internalizing and externalizing problem behaviour and reduced pro-social behaviour compared to children of parents using other parenting styles. In contrast, children with two authoritative parents showed the lowest levels of conduct problems. Hence, the above findings reinforced our results of authoritarian parenting leading to use of more avoidant coping strategies. Internalizing and externalizing problem behaviours are mostly due to avoidant coping strategies.

Donath, Graessel, Baier, Bleich and Hillemacher (2014), conducted a study on 44,610 class 9th students in Germany, to identify role of parenting styles in suicidal behaviour of adolescents. Results indicated that authoritative parenting protects against suicidal behaviour and was shown to lower the risk of suicide attempts by about 20%. This was the only protective factor that could be identified in the analyses. The results also show a relatively new result concerning the role of Rejecting-Neglecting parenting and suicidal thoughts and attempts. Having Rejecting-Neglecting parents increases the risk of suicide attempts in adolescents by more than 1.5 times.

Milevsky, Schlechter, Netter, and Keehn (2007), examined the adjustment of adolescents in relation to parents participation in a child's development with 272 adolescents studying in grade 9 and 11. This study was done through a survey supporting the claim that parenting styles are associated to adolescents' satisfaction. The survey was divided into two parts, one related to acceptance and involvement of a parent, and the second concerning strictness/ supervision. The results obtained through MANOVA indicated that authoritative parenting was associated with positive outcomes like higher self-esteem, more life-satisfaction, and lower depression. A significant difference between the permissive style, the authoritarian, and Neglectful style was also observed. The adolescents having permissive parents scored higher on self-esteem than the authoritarian and neglectful parents. They referred to studies suggesting that authoritative parenting, marked by patterns of warmth, non-punitive discipline, and consistency helps children develop several adaptive behaviours, in comparison to authoritarian styles, which are marked by patterns of low warmth, harsh discipline, and inconsistency, and permissive styles, characterised by low levels of supervision (Maccoby & Martin, 1983). They also stated that authoritative parenting has been shown to foster secure attachments between children and their caregiver leading to a greater sense of autonomy (Karavasilis, Doyle, & Markiewicz, 2003).

Torre-Cruz, Linares and Arias (2014), revealed from their study with 371 adolescents, that attribution of an authoritarian parenting style is related to manifestation of more aggressive and hostile behaviour toward peers, as compared to attribution of an authoritative or indulgent style. The perceived use of strict discipline is positively related to the different forms of aggressiveness, while a negative relationship is found with the affect dimension. They explained that the demand for obedience without discussion, typical of an authoritarian style, is linked to the exhibition of aggressive behaviours that may seriously impair adolescents' adjustment in different contexts, such as in peer interaction.

Okorodudu (2010), investigated the influence of parenting styles on adolescents' delinquency with 404 students. Regression analysis showed no significant relationship between authoritarian and authoritative parenting styles and adolescent delinquency, however, it showed significant relationship between laissez-faire parenting style and adolescents delinquency. They further described that Laissez-faire parenting dimension is without well-defined or clear-cut goals and such parents play passive role in child-rearing, which may lead to delinquent behaviour. In reference to our current study, inappropriate

However, a study was conducted by Thakre and Gupte (2016), on 261 adolescents within the age range of 13 to 15 years, to study the impact of parenting styles on aggression and emotional intelligence among adolescents. Results of ANOVA showed that there is no significant impact of parenting styles on aggression and emotional intelligence of the adolescents. Contrasting findings were attributed to small sample size, poor rapport during contact session and poor comprehension of the test items by the adolescents.

George et.al, (2018), conducted a cross-sectional study among 300 high school students, to assess emotional intelligence and parental bonding. Results of ANOVA reflected that there was no association between emotional intelligence and parenting style. The reason for contrasting findings was attributed to self-reporting measures of emotional intelligence. According to them, performance-based tests might have been a better measure of emotional intelligence.

Joshi & Dutta (2015), conducted a study on 246 class 10th students, to understand the correlation between parenting style and emotional intelligence of adolescents. Results of the correlation analysis showed that overall emotional intelligence was not significantly correlated with both mother's and father's parenting style. Additionally, the managing emotions dimension of emotional intelligence was negatively correlated with authoritative parenting. It was also found that a father's authoritarian parenting style was positively correlated with self-awareness aspect of emotional intelligence. They explained that although domination is a component of authoritarian style, however this control may be seen as involvement and concern in Asian cultures. In Indian families, conformity to cultural traditions and parental regulation is a normally expected behaviour in children and the findings are a reflection of Indian culture, where adolescents perceive parental strictness and demand for obedience as warmth and concern as opposed to the Western culture.

Gracia, Garcia and Lila (2008), analysed the relationships between parenting styles and adolescents' psychological adjustment with 489 Spanish children. MANOVA results suggest that adolescents of indulgent families do perform equal or even better in several indicators of psychological adjustment than adolescents from authoritative households. Authoritarian and neglectful parenting was associated, in general, with the minimum adjustment of adolescents. This suggests that the indulgent style of parenting, which according to our research is permissive parenting, can be considered as the optimum one. They explained that in the Spanish contexts parental warmth, acceptance and responsiveness are considered to be important for optimum psychological outcomes, whereas parental strictness and firm control may not be necessarily present.

A study by Bi et.al, (2018), with 633 adolescents, examined the relation between parenting styles and parent–adolescent relationship factors. Results of analysis of co-variance indicated that for all parenting styles, there were similar levels of parent–adolescent conflict frequency. This result may be credited to the traditional Asian culture, which emphasizes on maintaining pleasant relationships and avoiding confrontation (Peterson, Steinmetz, & Wilson, 2005). Additionally, the current study found that adolescents reported similar levels of conflict intensity with parents for both authoritative and authoritarian parenting styles. These findings are inconsistent with the previous findings, and this difference in results may be attributed to Asian culture, where adolescents may perceive the parents' intention to supervise their development positively, resulting in no direct relation between conflict intensity and levels of parental control. The current study also showed that adolescents with authoritative parents stated there were highest levels of cohesion, which is in sync with earlier studies. Authoritative parenting is described by high degree of warmth and acceptance along with supervision, but also includes the autonomy granting to adolescents' (Baumrind, 2005).

Hence, there are studies which show that authoritative parenting style has definite positive impact on emotional health of children. In our study, we are focusing on development of appropriate coping strategies like positive reappraisal and problem solving, which has been found to be more frequently used by children of authoritative parents as compared to authoritarian and permissive parents. There are studies which also show other parenting styles like authoritarian and permissive parenting styles to be better at developing optimum emotional health of children. Additionally, different studies show that authoritarian parenting style leads to problem behaviours and aggression in children. There are studies, which have found contrasting results too with regards to development of problem behaviours. However, in our study, results indicate that avoidant coping strategies like cognitive avoidance and acceptance and resignation are used more frequently by children of authoritarian parenting style as compared to authoritative and permissive parenting styles. The frequent use of avoidant coping strategies in the long run, can lead to aggression and/or problem behaviours due to denial in accepting the problems, pent up emotions and not being optimistic in solving problems. Therefore, it is important to teach children approach coping strategies to prepare them to handle bigger challenges in life.

In the present study, correlation between study habits and achievement motivation was found to be significant, which suggests that study habits and achievement motivation are positively related. This finding was supported by the study of Yazdani and Godbole (2014), who concluded from their research on 400 class 8th and 9th students, that study habits consisting of budgeting time, physical condition, reading ability, note taking, learning motivation, memory, taking examination and health, and achievement motivation have had significant relationship on academic performance. Students with good study habits and high achievement motivation had better academic performance. The study was conducted to study the relation of achievement motivation and study habits to academic performance in high school students. The correlation between learning motivation and study habits was also found to be significant.

Shelke (2019), in her research paper, discussing review of studies related to effective study habits for learners concluded that, effective learning depends on many factors and one of the important factor was motivation. She shared that effective learning depends on intelligence, intense and deep motivation, good physical health, stable home influences, fruitful guidance and instructions, emotional health of the learner, meaningful drills and repetition, concentration of effort, learning the whole, the meaningfulness of the situation, and its contact with the life of the learner.

A study was conducted on 400 students studying in 9th class to understand influence of achievement motivation, home environment, and study habits on academic achievement of secondary school students. Results showed that the correlation coefficients were significant at 0.01 level indicating a positive relation between achievement motivation and academic achievement, and study habits and academic achievement. The results also revealed the inter-correlations among the independent variables. There was a positive correlation between achievement motivation and home environment and achievement motivation and study habits (Vijayalakshmi, 1995).

A study by Turner, Chandler and Heffer (2009), with 264 undergraduate students supported previous research, which posits the relation between students being intrinsically motivated and academically successful. Although intrinsic motivation significantly predicted participants' academic performance, lack of motivation was also negatively associated students' performance.

However, in the study conducted by Siddiqui and Fatima (2014), with 278 grade 10 students, it was noted that the effect of achievement motivation on study habits and consequently on academic achievement was insignificant. The contrasting results were attributed to the minority sample used for the study. Hence, there are studies supporting our findings that study habits and achievement motivation are positively related, and good study habits are a result of having adequate motivation.

CHAPTER- VI

CONCLUSIONS, IMPLICATIONS & FUTURE RESEARCH

CONCLUSIONS

Overall, this study helped to solidify the previous findings that suggested the importance of parenting styles in child rearing. This study, helped us to focus on the impact of parenting on important variables of study habits and achievement motivation. Study habits and achievement motivation are extremely important for all students considering todays' competitive nature of the world. The research further brought attention to another important element of coping strategies and the effect of parenting styles on the same. Findings from the study showed that authoritative parenting style is the most effective style with regards to development of effective study habits and achievement motivation in adolescents. The results also revealed that authoritative parenting results in development of appropriate coping strategies in children. The authoritarian parenting leads to the development of inappropriate coping strategies like cognitive avoidance and acceptance, and resignation.

- This study shows that authoritative parents help build better study habits among their children when compared with authoritarian and permissive parenting styles. Authoritative parenting is characterized by involvement, nurturance, responsiveness, reasoning, and adequate autonomy granting. They are demanding and hence have high expectations of their children, which helps the children to set realistic goals for themselves. They themselves tend to be available and try to be good role models, which helps build necessary structure. They are responsive, thus, making them accessible to negotiate and discuss. These characteristics help parents to inculcate good study habits in children.

- The findings state that children of authoritarian parents have better study habits as compared to children of permissive parents. This shows that having high expectations from children and being demanding provides opportunity for children to follow them and succeed academically.
- The results of achievement motivation clearly show that adolescents with authoritative parents have high achievement motivation as compared to adolescents of authoritarian and permissive parents. Environment, which provides autonomy-supportive contexts enhance autonomous motivation, whereas, controlling contexts diminish autonomous motivation and enhance controlled motivation (Deci, Eghrari, Patrick, & Leone, 1994). Hence, parents who are responsive and provide proper guidance, have high hopes and set up rules, are flexible and supportive. This helps the children to develop adequate intrinsic motivation.
- The study mentioned no difference in achievement motivation of adolescents between authoritarian and permissive parenting styles. This provides insight into the need for adequate amounts of both demandingness and responsiveness for optimum development of motivation among children. Being demanding with no affection and understanding towards children, as well as, being only very

responsive with no limit setting can be detrimental for children and may lead to lack of motivation.

- Findings of the effect of parenting styles on development of coping with stress among adolescents pointed out that authoritative parenting style is most effective in developing appropriate approach coping strategies of positive reappraisal and problem solving when compared with authoritarian and permissive parenting styles. Providing supportive autonomy by authoritative parents, as well as, being available to provide assistance whenever required helps adolescents to be confident enough for approaching the problems; to brainstorm and practice solutions. Authoritative parents themselves being flexible, ready to negotiate, and adapt, help their children to develop socially adaptive behaviour leading to better psycho-social adjustment.
- Cognitive avoidance coping strategy, which is an avoidance coping strategy, was seen to be used more frequently by adolescents with authoritarian parenting style, followed by permissive parenting style; and least used by adolescents of authoritative parenting style. In this coping strategy, one avoids dealing with the stressor, sometimes even changing the perception of an experience completely. Authoritarian parents being rigid and highly directive may hamper developing a sense of mastery and confidence among their children making one to avoid any kind of stressor.

- Another avoidance coping strategy, that is, acceptance and resignation coping strategy, was found to be used more by children of authoritarian parents as compared to permissive and authoritative parenting styles. Here, one accepts the stressor and completely resigns to it thereby not making any effort to deal with it. Children of authoritarian parenting style become dependent on their parents as their parents often tend to dictate terms and expect total obedience. These children do not develop adequate problem solving skills or fear using any problem solving skills. This may lead to accepting the problem and resigning to the stressor.
- Correlation coefficient was calculated between study habits and achievement motivation of adolescents and it was found to be significantly positively related. This shows that as achievement motivation increases, adolescents tend to have and practice better study habits. This indicates that for an adolescent to practice effective study habits like time management, planning, reading to understand, memorize, and concentrate, one first needs to develop optimum achievement motivation.

RECOMMENDATIONS

- It was found that authoritative parenting style emerged as better for influencing positively in the area of study habits, motivation and coping with stress.
- Parents need to be responsive as well as nurturing, show involvement and sensitivity. They need to be reasonable, ready to negotiate, and encouraging. They need to direct the activities and decisions of their children through reasoning and discipline. They themselves need to be good role models especially in inculcating structure and following rules. This will help in fostering good study habits and adequate achievement motivation among adolescents thereby, leading to academic and overall success.
- Authoritative parenting style was found to be a positive influence for the growth of approach coping strategies, which in turn helps children have better psycho-social adjustment and develop resilience. Parents need to provide children with adequate opportunities of supportive autonomy to try different problem solving strategies, which will lead to improved self-efficacy and willingness to deal with any stressor.
- Hence, parents need to have a necessary balance between responsiveness and demandingness, and focus on being available and approachable to their children, as well as being acceptable of them.

- Teachers and educationists also need to encourage authoritative parenting through their interactions with parents to develop successful and happy individuals.

IMPLICATIONS

The different types of parenting styles are bound to have either favourable or adverse influence on the child's habits of studying and motivation. Parenting also has a huge impact on developing appropriate coping strategies. The changing times, competitive world, and easily available temptations or distractions are added challenges for personality development of a child. Hence, parenting holds utmost importance in the modern times. Therefore, keeping in mind the effect of parents and their styles on adolescents, this study has immense practical utility and social implications. Thus, this research would be of great use to psychologists, educational planners, institutional heads, and teachers along with parents and society.

- Psychologists/ counsellors can use this research to design parent and student workshops. Parents can be made aware of appropriate parenting practices, which will help them to be conscious parents. Parents can also be made aware of role modelling and their ability to transfer effective coping strategies to their children. Having adequate coping strategies are of utmost importance to any individual with ever increasing challenging life circumstances. Student workshops can focus on development of coping strategies and making them aware about the harmful effects of inappropriate coping strategies.

- Teachers can use this study to help students understand the importance of effective study habits to accomplish academic achievement. Teachers can also ignite intrinsic motivation among adolescents so that they study and achieve to feel good and not to gain only external rewards. Additionally, teachers can motivate parents to follow effective parenting practices to help parents become conscious parents.
- Educationists and educational planners can include importance of study habits in the curriculum to make students aware of the same. Stories on effective coping strategies can be included too to help adolescents learn about helpful coping strategies. This will also help reduce increasing suicide attempts among adolescents.
- Parents can learn appropriate parenting by engaging in parenting programs or workshops to help themselves and their children. This will lead to a resilient society, which will be able to bounce back after any stressors.

DIRECTIONS FOR FUTURE RESEARCH

Although, the current study contributes significantly to the knowledge of parenting, there is still much to be explored.

- Parenting styles of both parents can be explored with regards to the above variables. As more and more number of women are engaging in workforce, fathers are taking on an active role in parenting. Hence, studying fathers' parenting style may bring in additional insight into research of parenting.
- As parents have begun playing more active role as couples, with sharing of roles and financial responsibilities, understanding different joint parenting styles that exist and their influence on children can be studied. This can be very enlightening as effects of parenting are best studied in the family context and joint parenting styles can give us information regarding family atmosphere.
- Parenting may or may not get influenced by one's socio-economic background. Studying the effect of basic physiological and safety needs not being fulfilled and its impact on parenting can help us in understanding parenting in the context of basic struggles. This can help us understand the subsequent delinquent behaviour of children and the findings can help society in general.
- Comparative study of different socio-economic backgrounds can help us understand the difference in parenting styles that are prevalent. This can give insights into children's behaviour.

- Further studies examining the impact of differences in parenting styles can further explore how this affects the couple relationship and the child's perceptions of family support. Differences in parenting styles may impact the couple relationship in terms of disagreements over disciplining, disagreements in expectations and goals for the child, providing autonomy, etc. Differences in such parenting practices may also affect the parents' relationships with their child as the child may support one parent over the other based on his/her preferred parenting style. The child may also experience ambiguity about family rules, or the child may perceive less family cohesiveness. The relationship between these variables can be interesting and beneficial to clinicians, because it highlights prospective areas within the family structure to be addressed and resolved. These findings can specifically add to the literature of family therapy, which can help us in family counselling.
- Further research can also explore influence of peers, teachers, and other socializing agents on the development of children's coping styles. Research till date, in the area of coping, has mostly focussed on the influence of parenting, however, other environmental factors do play a significant role in children's emotional development. This will help counsellors in planning the systemic changes while helping to develop the coping strategies in children or adults.

LIMITATIONS

The current research study brought out the importance of parenting, however, there were few limitations.

- It was conducted in the area of Mumbai only, with schools catering to middle to upper middle class population. Hence, the results may not be applicable to students of BMC schools.
- Secondly, the low socio-economic background was not considered as an element of influence during the study, which might have influenced the variables studied. Hence, the effect of economic background on parenting practices, and the consequent impact on children cannot be understood by this study.
- In the parenting style, only the mothers' parenting style was considered, but, with increasing number of women engaged in work, fathers have begun playing an active role in child rearing. Hence, the influence of fathers' parenting style is unknown in the study. Additionally, any impact of joint parenting styles on the variables studied cannot be implied by the current findings.
- Lastly, the study did not cater to the students from IG and IB board who follow a different study method. Their study habits and motivation may have different factors and therefore, these findings cannot be completely generalised to them.

REFERENCES

REFERENCES

Abott-Chapman, J. A., Hughes, P. W., & Wyld, C. (1992). Monitoring student progress: A framework for improving student performance and reducing attrition in higher education [Paper presentation]. Youth Education Studies Centre, University of Tasmania: Hobart.

Abouserie, R. (1995). Self-esteem and achievement motivation as determinants of students' approaches to studying. *Studies in Higher Education*, *20*(1), 19-26

Accordino, D., Accordino, M., & Slaney, B. (2000). An investigation of perfectionism, mental health, achievement, and achievement motivation in adolescents. *Psychology in the Schools*, *37*(6), 535-545.

Acharya, N., & Joshi, S. (2009). Influence of Parents' Education on Achievement Motivation of Adolescents. *Indian Journal of Social Sciences*, *6*(1), 72-79.

Affrunti, N. W., & Ginsburg, G. S. (2012). Maternal over control and child anxiety: The mediating role of perceived competence. *Child Psychiatry & Human Development*, *43*(1), 102–112. https://doi: 10.1007/s10578-011-0248-z

Akbaş, A., & Kan, A. (2007). Affective Factors That Influence Chemistry Achievement (Motivation and Anxiety) and the Power of These Factors to Predict Chemistry Achievement-II. *Journal of Turkish Science Education*, *4*(1), 89-91.

Akca, C. (2012). Dogme Unplugged [Paper presentation]. First International Symposium on Language and Communication. Izmir, Turkey.

Albert, I., Trommsdorff, G., & Mishra, R. (2007). Parenting and adolescent attachment in India and Germany. In *Perspectives and progress in contemporary cross-cultural psychology*, 97–108. Beijing, China: Light Industry Press.

Albinhac, A. M. H., Jean, F. A. M., & Bouvard, M. P. (2018). Study of parental bonding in childhood in children and adolescents with anorexia nervosa. *Encephale*, *45*(2), 121–126. https://doi:10.1016/j.encep. 2018.02.004

Alderman, M. K. (1999). *Motivation for achievement*. New Jersey, United States: Lawrence Erlbaum.

Alimohamadi, N., Dehghani, M., & Saeide. (2018). Relation study between study habit and academic performance of nursing students in Hamadan. *Pajouhan Scientific Journal*, *16*(3), 29–38. https://doi: 10.21859/ psj.16.3.29

Alschuler, A. (1973). *Developing achievement motivation in adolescents*. New Jersey, United States: Educational Technology Publications.

Amabile, T. M. (1996). *Creativity in Context*. Boulder, Colorado: Westview.

Ames, C. (1992). Classrooms Goals Structures and Student Motivation. *Journal of Educational Psychology, 84*(3), 261-271. https://doi: 10.1037/0022-0663.84.3.261

Anderman, E. M., Griesinger, T., & Westerfield, G. (1998). Motivation and cheating during early adolescence. *Journal of Educational Psychology,* 90, 1-9.

Ang, R. P. (2006). Effects of parenting style on personal and social variables for Asian adolescents. *American Journal of Orthopsychiatry*, 76, 503-511.

Arenliu, A., Hoxha, L., Berxulli, D., & Gaṣhi, L. J. (2014). Parenting styles and intrinsic motivation among high school students - Do parenting styles influence motivation orientation of high school students? In 9th International Academic Conference, Istanbul, 38-46. https://doi: 10.13140/2.1.1433.9368

Arora, R. (2016). Academic achievement of adolescents in relation to study habits. *International Journal of Indian Psychology, 3*(9):48–54.

Ashish, R (2013). *Study Habits for Students: Bad Ones to Avoid, Good Ones to Achieve Success*. Retrived from www.education.wisc .education/soe/newsevents.

Aspelmeier, J. E., Love, M. M., McGill, L. A., Elliott, A. N., & Pierce, T. W. (2012). Self-esteem, locus of control, college adjustment, and GPA among first- and continuing-generation students: a moderator model of generational status. *Research in Higher Education, 53*(7), 755–781.

Assadi, S. M., Smetana, J., Shahmansouri, N., & Mohammadi, M. (2011). Beliefs about parental authority, parenting styles, and parent-adolescent conflict among Iranian mothers of middle adolescents. *International Journal of Behavioural Development*, 35, 424–431. https://doi: 10.1177/0165025411409121

Astin, A. (1999). Student involvement: a developmental theory for higher education. *Journal of College Student Development, 40*(5), 518–529.

Attaway, N. M., & Bry, B. H. (2004). Parenting Style and Black Adolescents' Academic Achievement. *Journal of Black Psychology, 30*(2), 229-247. Retrieved from https://doi.org/10.1177/0095798403260720

Atkinson, E. (1999). Key factors influencing pupil motivation in design and technology. Retrived from http://scholar.lib.vt.edu/ejournals/JTE/v10n2/atkindon.html.

Atkinson, J., & Feather, N. (1966). *A theory of achievement motivation*. New York: Wiley and Sons.

Austin, J. L., Lee, M. & Carr, J. P. (2003). The effects of guided notes on undergraduate students' recording of lecture content. *Journal of Instructional Psychology, 31*(4).

Ausubel, D. A. (1968). *Educational psychology: A cognitive view*. New York, United States: Holt, Rinehart & Winston.

Awan, R., Noureen, G., & Naz, A. (2011). A Study of Relationship between Achievement Motivation, Self-Concept and Achievement in English and Mathematics at Secondary Level. *International Education Studies, 4*(3), 40-52.

Bacanli, H. (2002). Behaviorist Approach. In Kaya, Z., & Akdemir, A. S. (1st edition). *Learning and Teaching Theories, Approaches and Models*. Ankara, Turkey: Cozum

Bae, S. (2015). The relationships between perceived parenting style, learning motivation, friendship satisfaction, and the addictive use of smartphones with elementary school students of South Korea: Using multivariate latent growth modelling. *School Psychology International*, *36*(5). https://doi: 10.1177/0143034315604017.

Bahr, S. J., & Hoffmann, J. P. (2010). Parenting style, religiosity, peers, and adolescent heavy drinking. *Journal of Studies on Alcohol and Drugs*, *71*(4), 539–543. https://doi:10.15288/jsad.2010.71.539

Bailey, T. H., & Phillips, L. J. (2016). The influence of motivation and adaptation on students' subjective well-being, meaning in life and academic performance. *Higher Education Research and Development*, *35*(2), 201–216.

Baker, R. W., & Siryk, B. (1984). Measuring adjustment to college. *Journal of Counseling Psychology*, *31*(2), 179–189.

Balda, S., Irving, K., Berthelsen, D., & Catherwood, D. (2001). Parental control and style in Australia and India: A cross-cultural study. *Journal of Human Ecology, 12*(2), 133–139. https://doi: 10.1080/09709274. 2001.11907593

Balkis, M., Erdinç, D., & Buluş, M. (2012). Analysis of the relation between academic procrastination, academic rational/irrational beliefs, time preferences to study for exams, and academic achievement: A structural model. *European Journal of Psychology of Education, 28*(3), 2-5. https://doi:10.1007/s10212-012-0142-5.

Bamman, H. A. (1954). Study skills program Sanford University *California Journal of Educational Research*, 5, 57-58.

Bandura, A. (1997). *Self-efficacy: The exercise of control.* New York, United States: W. H. Freeman

Barber, B. K., Stolz, H. E., Olsen, J. A., Collins, W. A., & Burchinal, M. (2005). Parental support, psychological control, and behavioral control: Assessing relevance across time, culture, and method. *Monographs of the society for research in child development*, 70, 120-147.

Barnhart, C. M., Raval, V. V., Jansari, A., & Raval, P. H. (2013). Perceptions of parenting style among college students in India and the United States. *Journal of Child and Family Studies, 22*(5), 684-693. https://doi: 10.1007/s10826-012-9621-1

Barnes, G. M., & Farrell, M. P. (1992). Parental support and control as predictors of adolescent drinking, delinquency, and related problem behaviors. *Journal of Marriage and the Family*, 54, 763-776. https://doi: 10.2307/353159.

Barrett, P., Shortt, A., & Healy, L. (2002). Do parent and child behaviours differentiate families whose children have obsessive-compulsive disorder from other clinic and non-clinic families? *Journal of Child Psychology and Psychiatry, 43*(5), 597-607. https://doi.org/10.1111/1469-7610.00049

Barton, & Hirsch. (2015). Permissive Parenting and Mental Health in College Students: Mediating Effects of Academic Entitlement. *Journal of American College Health*, 23-37. https://doi: 10.1080/07448481.2015.1060597.

Bashir, I., & Mattoo, N. H. (2012). A study on study habits and academic performance among adolescents (14-19) years. *International Journal of Social Science Tomorrow*, *1*(5), 220-231.

Bassett, J. F., Snyder, T. L., Roger, D. T., & Collins, C.L. (2013). Permissive, authoritarian, and authoritative instructors: Applying the concept of parenting styles to the college classroom. *Individual Differences Research*, 11, 1-11.

Baumrind, D., Larzelere, R, E., Owens, E, B. (2010). Effects of Preschool Parents' Power Assertive Patterns and Practices on

Adolescent Development. *Science and Practice, 10*(3), 157-201. https://doi: 10.1080/15295190903290790

Baumrind, D. (2005). Patterns of parental authority and adolescent autonomy. *New directions for child and adolescent development, 61*(9), 108-109. https://doi: 10.1002/cd.128.

Baumrind, D. (1997). The discipline controversy revisited. *Family Relations*, 45, 405 - 414.

Baumrind, D. (1991). The influence of parenting style on adolescent competence and substance use. *The Journal of Early Adolescence, 11*(1), 56-95.

Baumrind, D. (1971). Child care practices anteceding three patterns of preschool behaviour. *Genetic Psychology Monographs, 75*(1), 43-88.

Baumrind, D. (1967). Child care practices anteceding three patterns of pre-school behavior. *Genetic Psychology Monographs, 75*(1), 43-88.

Bean, R. A., Barber, B. K., & Crane, D. R. (2006). Parental support, behavioral control, and psychological control among African American youth: The relationships to academic grades, delinquency, and depression. *Journal of Family Issues*, 27, 1335-1355. https://doi: 10.1177/0192513X06289649.

Berg, B. (2011). The effects of parenting styles on a preschool aged child's social emotional development. Doctoral thesis submitted to The Graduate School, University of Winsconsin-Stout.

Retrieved from http://www2.uwstout.edu/content/lib/thesis/2011/2011bergb.pdf.

Bharadwaj, R. L. (1997). Development of parenting scale. *Indian Journal of psychometry and education, 26*(2), 109-112.

Bhattacharyya, P., & Pradhan, R. K. (2015). Perceived paternal parenting style and proactive coping strategies of Indian adolescents. *International Journal of Psychological Studies, 7*(2), 180-182. https://doi: 10. 5539/ijps.v7n2p180

Bi, X., Yang, Y., Li, H., Wang, M., Zhang, W., & Deater-Deckard, K. (2018). Parenting Styles and Parent–Adolescent Relationships: The Mediating Roles of Behavioral Autonomy and Parental Authority, *Frontiers in Psychology*, 9, 2187-2199. https://doi.org/10.3389/fpsyg.2018.02187

Boggiano, A. K., Shields, A., Barrett, M., Kellam, T., Thompson, E., Simons, J., & Katz, P (1992). Helpless deficits in students: The role of motivational orientation. *Motivation and Emotion, 16*(3), 271-296.

Boon, H. J. (2007). *Family, motivational and behavioural links to Indigenous Australian Adolescents' achievement.* Paper presented at AARE Annual Conference in Fremantle, University of Notre Dame. Retrieved from http://eprints.jcu.edu.au/2048/1/boo07027.pdf.

Bong, M., & Skaalvik, E. M. (2003). Academic self-concept and self-efficacy: How different are they really? *Educational Psychology Review, 15*(1), 1-40.

Bornstein, M. H., & Zlotnik, D. (2008). Parenting styles and their effects. *Encyclopedia of Infant and Early Childhood Development*, 496-509.

Bornstein, M. H. (2012). Cultural approaches to parenting. *Parenting, Science and Practice, 12*(2-3), 212–221. https://doi:10.1080/15295192.2012.683359

Br, S., & Manohari, S., & Raman, V. (2019). Parenting styles and its impact on children – a cross cultural review with a focus on India. *Mental Health, Religion & Culture*, 1-27. https://doi:10.1080/13674676.2019.1594178.

Bradley, R.H. (2007). Parenting in the breach: How parents help children cope with developmentally challenging circumstances. *Parenting: Science and Practice, 7,* 99-148.

Brooks, F. D., & Heston, T. C. (1945). The validity of items in a study habits inventory. *Journal of Educational Psychology*, 36, 257-270.

Brooks, J. B. (1991). *The process of parenting*. Mayfield, California: Palo Alto.

Bronstein, P., Ginsburg, G. S., & Herrera, I. S. (2005). Parental predictors of motivational orientation in early adolescence: A longitudinal study. *Journal of Youth and Adolescence, 34*(6), 559–575. https://doi:10. 1007/s10964-005-8946-0

Brown, L., & Iyengar, S. (2008). Parenting Styles: The Impact on Student Achievement. *Marriage and Family Review, 43* (1), 14-38.

https://doi: 10.1080/01494920802010140.

Brown, H. D. (2007). *Principles of Language Learning and Teaching, 5th edition.* White Plains, New York: Pearson Education Inc.

Bruner, J. (1966). *Toward a theory of instruction*. Cambridge, Massachusetts: Harvard University Press.

Buri, J. (1992). Parental Authority Questionnaire. *Journal of Personality Assessment,* 57(1), 110-119

Burlison, J. D., Murphy, C. S., & Dwyer, W. O. (2009). Evaluation of the motivated strategies for learning questionnaire for predicting academic performance in college students of varying scholastic aptitude. *College Student Journal, 43*(4), 1313–1323.

Burnett, Collins, W. (1951). Study skills and counsellor training. A two way teaching programme. *California Journal of Educational Research*, 2, 18-21.

Bush, K. R., & Peterson, G. W. (2013). *Parent-child relationships in diverse contexts*, Handbook of Marriage and the Family, 3rd edn, 275–302. New York, NY: Springer. https://doi: 10.1007/978-1-4614-3987-5_13

Butterweck. (1957). *How to study*. New York: McGraw –Hill Book Company.

Bynum, M.S., & Brody, G.H. (2005). Coping behaviors, parenting, and perceptions of children's internalizing and externalizing problems in rural African American mothers. *Family Relations, 54,* 58-71.

Calafat, A., García, F., Juan, M., Becoña, E., & Fernández-Hermida, J. R. (2014). Which parenting style is more protective against adolescent substance use? Evidence within the European context. *Drug and Alcohol Dependence*, 138, 185–192. https://doi:10.1016/j.drugalcdep.2014.02.705

Calkins, S.D. (1994). Origins and outcomes of individual differences in emotion regulation. *Monographs of the Society for Research in Child Development, 59*, 53-72.

Campbell, A., & Ntobedzi, A. (2007). Emotional Intelligence, Coping and Psychological Distress: A Partial Least Squares Approach to Developing a Predictive Model. *E-Journal of Applied Psychology,* 3(2). https://doi:10.7790/ejap.v3i2.91.

Carter, H. D. (1950). Correlation between intelligence test, study methods test and marks in a college course. *Journal of Psychology*, 30, 333-340.

Catherine, M. C. & Lei, C. (1998). Adolescent-parent relations in Hong Kong: parenting styles, emotional autonomy, and school achievement. Journal of Genetic Psychology, 159, 421–436.

Chan, T. W., & Koo, A. (2010). Parenting style and youth outcomes in the UK. *European Sociological Review*, 1-15. http://users.ox.ac.uk/~sfos0006/papers/esr2010.pdf

Chand, S. (2013).Study habits of secondary school students in relation to type of school and type of family. *International Journal of Social Science & Interdisciplinary Research*, *2*(7), 48-55.

Chatzisarantis, N., & Hagger, M. (2009). Effects of an intervention based on self-determination theory on self-reported leisure-time physical activity participation. *Psychology & health*, *24* (1), 29-48. https://doi:10.1080/08870440701809533.

Chemers, M. M., Hu, L., & Garcia, B. F. (2001). Academic self-efficacy and first year college student performance and adjustment. *Journal of Educational Psychology, 93*(1), 55-64.

Chen, Q. D., & Zhou, H. (1997). Authoritative and authoritarian parenting practices and social and school performance in Chinese children. *International Journal of Behavioral Development*, 21, 855-873.

Chen, B., Vansteenkiste, M., Beyers, W., Soenens, B., & Petegem, S. V. (2013). Autonomy in family decision making for Chinese adolescents: disentangling the dual meaning of autonomy. *Journal of Cross Cultural Psychology*, 44, 1184–1209. https://doi: 10.1177/0022022113480038

Chowdhury, S., & Ghose, A. (2014). Effects of Patterns of Parenting on Study Habits of Adolescents. *International Journal of Humanities and Social Science Invention, 3*(3), 15-19.

Clark, R. M. (1993). *Homework-focused parenting practices that positively affect student achievement.* In Families and Schools in a Pluralistic Society, 85-105. Albany: State University of New York Press.

Clarke, K., Cooper, P., & Creswell, C. (2013). The parental overprotection scale: Associations with child and parental anxiety. Journal of Affective Disorders, *151*(2), 618–624. https://doi:10.1016/j.jad.2013.07.007

Cohen, S., & Wills, T. A. (1985). Stress, social support, and the buffering hypothesis. *Psychological Bulletin*, *98*(2), 310-357. http://dx.doi.org/10.1037/0033-2909.98.2.310

Coleman, M. F. (1993). The role of parental interaction in achievement motivation. *The Journal of Social Psychology*, 133, 859-861.

Collins, W. A., Maccoby, E. E., Steinberg, L., Hetherington, E. M., & Bornstein, M. H. (2000). Contemporary research on parenting: The case for nature and nurture. *American Psychologist*, *55*(2), 218–232. https://doi:10.1037/0003-066X.55.2.218

Compas, B.E., Forehand, R., Thigpen, J, C., Keller, G., Hardcastle, E, J., Cole, D, A.,... Roberts, L. (2011). Family group cognitive-behavioral preventive intervention for families of depressed parents: 18- and 24-month outcomes. *Journal of Consulting and Clinical Psychology, 79*(4), 488-499. https://doi:10.1037/a0024254

Compas, B. E., Boyer, M. C., Stanger, C., Colletti, R. B., Thomsen, A. H., Dufton,, L. M., & Cole, D. A. (2006a). Latent variable analysis of coping, anxiety/depression, and somatic symptoms in adolescents with chronic pain. *Journal of Consulting and Clinical Psychology,* 74, 1132-1142.

Compas, B. E. (2006b). Measurement of coping and stress responses in women with breast cancer. *Psycho-Oncology,* 15, 1038-1054.

Compas, B. E., Connor-Smith, J. K., Saltzman, H., Thomsen, A. H., & Wadsworth, M. E. (2001). Coping with stress during childhood and adolescence: problems, progress, and potential in theory and research. *Psychological Bulletin,* 127, 87-127.

Connor-Smith, J. K., Compas, B. E., Wadsworth, M. E., Thomsen, A. H., & Saltzman, H. (2000). Responses to stress in adolescence: Measurement of coping and involuntary stress responses. *Journal of Consulting and Clinical Psychology,* 68, 976-992.

Creekmore. (2010). Intrinsic Motivation and its effects on Student Academic Achievement. [Paper presentation]. Education Articles: School Improvement. http://www.edarticle.com/articles/1040/intrinsic-motivation-and-its-effectson- student-academic-achievement.

Credé, M., & Phillips, L. A. (2011). A meta-analytic review of the motivated strategies for learning questionnaire. *Learning and Individual Differences, 21*(4), 337–346.

Crede, M., & Kuncel, N. (2008). Study Habits, Skills, and Attitudes: The Third Pillar Supporting Collegiate Academic Performance. *Perspectives on Psychological Science, 3*(6), 425-453. https://doi.org/10.1111%2Fj.1745-6924.2008.00089.x

Cummings, E. M., Davies, P. T., Campbell, S.B. (2000). *Developmental Psychopathology and Family Process*. New York, NY: The Guilford Press.

Cusimano*,* J.T. (1999). *Study skills for a successful semester*. Black Collegian, New Orleans: 30(1).

Darling, N., Cumsille, P., & Martínez, M. L. (2008). Individual differences in adolescents' beliefs about the legitimacy of parental authority and their own obligation to obey: a longitudinal investigation. *Child Development*, 79, 1103–1118. https://doi: 10.1111/j.1467-8624.2008.01178.x

Darling, N., Cumsille, P., & Martínez, M. L. (2007). Adolescents' as active agents in the socialization process: legitimacy of parental authority and obligation to obey as predictors of obedience. Journal of Adolescence, 30, 297–311. https://doi: 10.1016/j.adolescence.2006.03.003

Darling, N., Cumsille, P., & Peña-Alampay, L. (2005). Rules, legitimacy of parental authority, and obligation to obey in Chile, the Philippines, and the United States. *New Directions for Child and Adolescent Development*, 47–60. https://doi: 10.1002/cd.127

Darling, N., & Steinberg, L. (1993). Parenting style as context: An integrative model. *Psychological Bulletin, 13*(3), 487-496.

Deci, E. L., & Ryan, R. M. (2000). Self-determination theory and the facilitation of intrinsic motivation, social development, and wellbeing. *American Psychologist,* 55(1), 68-78.

Deci, E. L., Eghrari, H., Patrick, B. C., & Leone, D. R. (1994). Facilitating internalization: The self-determination perspective. *Journal of Personality, 62,* 119-142.

Deci, E. L., Vallerand, R. J., Pelletier, L. G., & Ryan, R. M. (1991). Motivation and education: The self-determination perspective. The Educational Psychologist, 74, 852-859.

Deci, E. L., & Ryan, R. (1985). *Intrinsic motivation and self-determination in human behavior.* New York, United States: Plenum.

Deci, V., Simons, L., & Sheldon. (2004). Motivating Learning, Performance, and Persistence: The Synergistic Effects of Intrinsic Goal Contents and Autonomy-Supportive Contexts. *Journal of Personality and Social Psychology*, *87*(2), 246–260. https://doi: 10.1037/0022-3514.87.2.246

Decharms, Richard (1984). Motivation Enhancement in Educational Settings. In *Research on Motivation in Education, Student Motivation,* 1. New York, NY: Academic Press.

De Clercq, M., Galand, B., Dupont, S., & Frenay, M. (2013). Achievement among first-year university students: an integrated and contextualized approach. *European Journal of Psychology of Education, 28*(3), 641–662.

Deo, P. and Mohan, A. (2011). Manual for achievement motivation scale. Agra, India: National Psychological Corporation, 1-10.

Diener, C. L. (1960). Similarities and Differences between Over-Achieving and Under-Achieving Students. *The Personnel and Guidance Journal, 38*(5), 396-400. https://doi.org/10.1002/j.2164-4918.1960.tb02570.x

Dil, S., & Bulantekin, O. (2011). Determination of the relationship between family functionality and locus of control and levels of academic success among nursing students. *Journal of Psychiatric Nursing, 2*(1), 17-24.

Diseth, A., & Kobbeltvedt, T. (2010). A mediation analysis of achievement motives, goals, learning strategies, and academic achievement. *The British Journal of educational psychology,* 80, 671-687. https://doi:10.1348/000709910X492432.

Dittman, C. K., Keown, L. J., Sanders, M. R., Rose, D., Farrugia, S.P., & Sofronoff, K. (2011). An epidemiological examination of parenting and family correlates of emotional problems in young children. *The American Journal of Orthopsychiatry*, 81(3), 360–371. https://doi: 10.1111/j.1939-0025.2011.01104.x.

Dixon, S. V., Graber, J. A., & Brooks-Gunn, J. (2008). The roles of respect for parental authority and parenting practices in parent-child conflict among African American, Latino, and European American families. *Journal of Family Psychology*, *22*(1), 1–10. https://doi: 10.1037/0893-3200.22.1.1

Donath, C., Graessel, E., Baier, D., Bleich, S., & Hillemacher, T. (2014). Is parenting style a predictor of suicide attempts in a representative sample of adolescents? *BMC Pediatrics*, *14*(1), 113. https://doi: 10. 1186/1471-2431-14-113

Dornbusch, S. M., Ritter, P. L., Leiderman, P., Roberts, D. F., & Fraleigh, M. J. (1987). The relation of parenting style to adolescent school performance. *Child Development*, 58, 1244-1257.

Dowson, M., & McInerney, D. M. (2001). Psychological parameters of students' social and work avoidance goals: A qualitative investigation. *Journal of Educational Psychology, 93*(1), 35-42.

Driscoll, A., Russell, S., & Crockett, L. (2008). Parenting Styles and Youth Well-Being across Immigrant Generations. *Journal of Family Issues, 29* (2), 185-209. https://doi: 10.1177/0192513X07307843.

D'souza, G., & Mendes, J. (2014). A Comparative Study of the Two Dimensions of Parenting Style and their Effects on the Self-

Concept of Pre-Adolescents. *The International Journal of Indian Psychology, 2*(1), 24-34. Retrieved from http://www.academia.edu/11116844

Dupeyrat, C., & Marine, C. (2005). Implicit theories of intelligence, goal orientation, cognitive engagement, and achievement: A test of Dweck's model with returning to school adults. *Contemporary Educational Psychology, 30* (1), 43-59.

Dwairy, M., & Menshar, K. E. (2005). Parenting style, individuation, and mental health of Egyptian adolescents. *Journal of Adolescence, 29*, 103-117. https://doi:10.1016/j.adolescence.2005.03.002

Dweck, C. S., & Leggett, E. L., (1988). A Social-cognitive approach to motivation and personality. *Psychological Review, 95*(2), 256-273. https://doi.org/10.1037/0033-295X.95.2.256

Ebele, U., & Olofu, P. (2017). Study habit and its impact on secondary school students' academic performance in biology in the Federal Capital Territory, Abuja. *Educational Research and Reviews, 12*(10), 583-588. https://doi:10.5897/ERR2016.3117.

Edwards, C. D. (1999). How to handle a hard-to handle kid: A parents' guide to understanding and changing problem behaviors. Minneapolis, United States: Free Spirit Publishing.

Eisenberg, N., Spinrad, T.L., & Eggum, N.D. (2010). Emotion-related self-regulation and its relation to children's maladjustment. *Annual Review of Clinical Psychology, 6*,495-525.

Eisenberg, N., Cumberland, A., & Spinrad, T.L. (1998). Parental socialization of emotion. *Psychological Inquiry, 9*(4), 241-273.

Eisenberg, N., Fabes, R.A., & Murphy, B. (1996). The relations of child dispositional empathy-related responding to their emotionality, regulation, and social functioning. *Developmental Psychology, 32*(2), 195-209.

Ekeke, H., & Telu, J. (2013). Influence of home on study habits of secondary school Students in Kalo-Creek development centre of Bayelsa state, Nigeria. *American Journal of Secondary Education*, *1*(1), 1-6.

Elham, D., Siti, N.Y., Rumaya,B.J., & Mansor, A.T. (2012). Relationship between parenting style and academic achievement among Iranian adolescents in Sirjan. *Asian Social Science, 8*(1), 156-160.

Elias, H., & Yee, T.H. (2009). Relationship between perceived paternal and maternal parenting styles and students' academic achievement in selected secondary schools. *European Journal of Social Sciences*, *9*(2), 181-192.

Eliot, L., Foster, S., & Stinson, M. (2002). Student study habits using notes from a speech to-text support service*, Exceptional Children, 69*(1), 25-40.

Elliot, A. J., & McGregor H. A. (2001). A 2x2 achievement goal framework. *Journal of Personality and Social Psychology, 80*(3), 501-519.

Enten, R. S., & Golan, M. (2009). Parenting styles and eating disorder pathology. *Appetite, 52*(3), 784– 787. https://doi:10.1016/j.appet.2009.02.013

Eschenbeck, C. W., Kohlmann, & Lohaus, A. (2007). Gender differences in coping strategies in children and adolescents, *Journal of Individual Differences, 28*(1), 18-26.

Eun, J. D., Paksarian, D., He, J. P., & Merikangas, K. R. (2018). Parenting style and mental disorders in a nationally representative sample of US adolescents. *Social Psychiatry and Psychiatric Epidemiology, 53*(1), 11–20. https://doi:10.1007/s00127-017-1435-4

Faravelli, C., Di, P. F., Scarpato, M. A., & Fioravanti, G. (2010). Parental attitudes of mothers of patients with panic disorder. *Journal of Psychopathology*, 16, 144–149. https://pdfs.semanticscholar.org/e78f/8a9102866587ee2bbd5d70b034182ccc1fb1.pdf

Finkenauer, C., Engels, R., & Baumeister, R. F. (2005). Parenting behaviour and adolescent behavioural and emotional problems: The role of self-control. *International Journal of Behavioral Development, 29*(1), 58-69. https://doi.org/10.1080%2F01650250444000333

Folkman, S., & Lazarus, R. S. (1980). An analysis of coping in a middle-aged community sample. *Journal of Health and Social Behaviour, 21*(3), 219-239.

Fontana, D. (1981). *Psychology for Teachers*. London, England: Macmillan Press Ltd.

Fonte, B. A. (2015). Relationship between parenting style, emotional intelligence and self-esteem. Thesis submitted to Washington College. Retrieved from: http://hdl.handle.net/10090/7271.

Fuligni, A. J. (1998). Authority, autonomy, and parent-adolescent conflict and cohesion: a study of adolescents from Mexican, Chinese, Filipino, and European backgrounds. *Developmental Psychology, 34*(4), 782–792. https://doi: 10.1037/0012-1649.34.4.782

Gafoor, & Kurukkan. (2014). Construction and Validation of Scale of Parenting Style. *Journal of Behavioral and Social Sciences, 2*(4), 315-321.

Galambos, N. L., Barker, E. T., Almeida, D. M. (2003). Parents do matter: trajectories of change in externalizing and internalizing problems in early adolescence. *Child Development, 74*(2); 578–594. https://doi: 10.1111/1467-8624.7402017.

Gar, N. S., Hudson, J. L., & Rapee, R. M. (2005). Family factors and the development of anxiety disorders. In J. L. Hudson & R. M. Rapee (Eds.), *Psychopathology and the family* (125–145). New York, NY: Elsevier Science.

Gardner, R. A., & Gardner, B. T. (1978). Comparative psychology and language acquisition. *Annals of the New York Academy of*

Sciences, 309 (1), 37-76. https://doi.org/10.1111/j.1749-6632.1978.tb29441.x

George, N., George, M., Goud, R., Shaju, A., Johnson, R., Mathew, T, P., Golapalli, C., & Shanbhag, D. (2018). A study of emotional intelligence and perceived parenting styles among adolescents in a rural area in Karnataka. *Journal of Family Medicine and Primary Care, 6*(4), 848-852. https://doi: 10.4103/jfmpc.jfmpc_100_17.

Gracia, E., & Garcia, F., & Lila, M. (2008). What Is Best for Your Children? Authoritative vs. Indulgent Parenting Styles and Psychological Adjustment of Spanish Adolescents [Paper presentation]. *In International congress on interpersonal acceptance and rejection*, Istanbul, Turkey, 113-124.

Garg, R., Levin, E., Urajnik, D., & Kauppi, C. (2005). Parenting style and academic achievement for East Indian and Canadian adolescents. *Journal of Comparative Family Studies, 36*(4), 653–661. https://doi:10.3138/jcfs.36.4.653

Gentzler, A.L., Contreras-Grau, J.M., Kerns, K.A., & Weimer, B.L. (2005). Parent-child emotional communication and children's coping in middle childhood. *Social Development, 14*(4), 591-612.

Glasgow, K., Dornbusch, S., Troyer, L., Steinberg, L., & Ritter, P. (1997). Parenting Styles, Adolescents' Attributions, and Educational Outcomes in Nine Heterogeneous High

Schools. *Child Development, 68*(3), 507-529. https://doi:10.2307/1131675

Glenn, R.E. (2003). Study skills to help kids use time wisely [online article]. *In The Education Digest, 69*(3), (51), *Ann Arbor:* Ebscohost connection.

Gonzalez, A. L., & Wolters, C. A. (2006). The relation between perceived parenting practices and achievement motivation in mathematics. *Journal of Research in Childhood Education*, 21, 203- 217.

Gonzalez, A. R., Holbein, M. F. D., & Quilter, S. (2002). High school students' goal orientations and their relationship to perceived parenting styles. *Contemporary Educational Psychology, 27*(3), 450-470.

Gotta, A. (2012). Effects of parenting styles, academic self-efficacy, and achievement motivation on the academic achievement of university students in Ethiopia. *Doctoral thesis submitted to Edith Cowan University*. https://ro.ecu.edu.au/theses/461

Gottfried, A.E., Fleming, J.S., & Gottfried, A.W. (1994). Role of parental motivational practices in children's academic intrinsic motivation and achievement. *Journal of Educational Psychology*, 86, 104-113.

Grace F (20 13). Would Group Study Improve Your Grades? Retrieved from www.about.com.

Graham, S., & Weiner, B. (1996). Theories and principles of motivation. In Berliner, D. C., & Calfee, R. C (Ed.), *Handbook of educational psychology* (p. 63-84). Macmillan Library Reference, USA: Prentice Hall International.

Gray, M. R., & Steinberg, L. (1999). Unpacking authoritative parenting: Reassessing a multidimensional construct. *Journal of Marriage and the Family, 61*(3), 574–587. https://doi: 10.2307/353561

Greene, B. A., & Miller, R. B. (1996). Influences on achievement: Goals, perceived ability, and cognitive engagement. *Contemporary Educational Psychology, 21*(2), 181-192. https://doi:10.1006/ceps.1996.0015

Grolnik, W.S., & Farkas, M. (2002). Parenting and the development of children's self-regulation. In Bornstein, M.H. (Ed.), Handbook of parenting, *5, Practical issues in parenting* (p. 89-110). Mahwah, NJ: Lawrence Erlbaum Associates.

Grolnick, W., & Ryan, R. (1989). Parent Styles Associated with Children's Self-Regulation and Competence in School: using a structured interview. *Journal of Educational Psychology, 81*(2), 143-154. https://doi:10.1037/0022-0663.81.2.143.

Guay, F., Marsh, H. W., & Boivin, M. (2003). Academic self-concept and academic achievement: Developmental perspectives on their causal ordering. *Journal of Educational Psychology, 95*(1), 124-136.

Gullotta, T. P., Blau, G. M., & Ramos, J. M. (2007). *Handbook of childhood behavioural issues: Evidence-based approaches to prevention and treatment.* London, England: CRC Press.

Gunderson, E. A., Donnellan, M. B., Robins, R. W., & Trzesniewski, K. H. (2018). The specificity of parenting effects: Differential relations of parent praise and criticism to children's theories of intelligence and learning goals. *Journal of Experimental Child Psychology,* 173, 116–135. https://doi:10.1016/j.jecp.2018.03.015.

Hallas, C. H. (2002). *The Core and Training of the Mentally Retarded. Bristol,* England: Bristol John Wright and Sons.

Harpe, T., & Row, A. (2009). Effective Study Habits. Retrieved from www.arbeitsblaetter.com.

Havighurst, S. S., Wilson, K. R., Harley, A. E., & Prior, M. R. (2009). Tuning in to kids: An emotion-focused parenting program – initial findings from a community trial. *Journal of Community Psychology, 37*(8), 1008-1023.

Hazen, E., Schlozman, S., & Beresin, E. (2008). Adolescent Psychological Development: A Review. *Pediatrics in review, 29*(5), 161-168. https://doi:10.1542/pir.29-5-161.

Heaven, P.C.L., & Joseph, C. (2008). Parental styles, conscientiousness, and academic performance in high school: a three-wave longitudinal study. *Psychological Bulletin, 34*(4), 451–461.

Hendrickson, A. B. (1997). Predicting student success with the Learning and Study Strategies Inventory (LASSI). Master's thesis submitted to Iowa State University, Ames, IA.

Hepher, H.W. (1990). *Psychology Applied to Life and Work*. London, England: Pan Books Ltd.

Hills, P.S., & Ballow, H. (2000). *Effective Study Skill*. London, England: Pan Books Ltd.

Hirata, H., & Kamakura, T. (2018). The effects of parenting styles on each personal growth initiative and self-esteem among Japanese university students. *International Journal of Adolescence and Youth, 23*(3), 325-333.

Hoang, T. N. (2007). The relations between parenting and adolescent motivation. *International Journal of Whole Schooling, 3*(2), 1-21.

Hoeve, M., Blokland, A., Dubas, J. S., Loeber, R., Gerris, J. R. M., & Van der Laan, P. H. (2008). Trajectories of delinquency and parenting styles. *Journal of Abnormal Child Psychology*, 36, 223–235.

Hoeve, M., Dubas, J. S., Gerris, J. R., Van der Laan, P. H., & Smeenk, W. (2011). Maternal and paternal parenting styles: Unique and combined links to adolescent and early adult delinquency. *Journal of Adolescence, 34*(5), 813–827.

Huang, C. Y., Cheah, C. S., Lamb, M. E., & Zhou, N. (2017). Associations between parenting styles and perceived child effortful control within Chinese families in the United States, the United Kingdom, and Taiwan. *Journal of Cross-Cultural Psychology, 48*(6), 795–812. https://doi:10.1177/0022022117706108

Hurtado, S., Han, J. C., Sáenz, V. B., Espinosa, L. L., Cabrera, N. L., & Cerna, O. S. (2007). Predicting transition and adjustment to college: biomedial and behavioral science aspirants' and minority students' first year of college. *Research in Higher Education, 48*(7), 841–887.

Husain, A. (2000). Developing Study Habits. Wikipedia: the free encyclopedia.

Huver, R. M. E., Otten, R., Vries, H. de., & Engels, R. C. M. E. (2009). Personality and parenting style in parents of adolescents. *Journal of Adolescence,* 33, 395-402. Retrieved, from ScienceDirect database.

Jacob, P., & Seshadri, S. P. (2013). Parenting in children and adolescents with internalising disorders. *Journal of Indian Association for Child and Adolescent Mental Health, 9*(4), 136–148. Retrieved from http://www.jiacam.org/0904/reviewoct2013.pdf

Jacobsen, W. C., & Forste, R. (2011). The wired generation: academic and social outcomes of electronic media use among university students. *Cyber psychology, Behavior and Social Networking, 14*(5), 275–280.

Jaffee, M., Gullone, E., & Hughes, E. K. (2010). The roles of temperamental dispositions and perceived parenting behaviors in the use of two emotion regulation strategies in late childhood. *Journal of Applied Developmental Psychology,* 31*,* 47-59.

Jagacinski, C. M., &Duda, J. L. (2001). A comparative analysis of contemporary achievement goal orientation measures. *Educational and Psychological Measurement, 61*(6), 1013-1039. https://doi:10.1177/00131640121971626

Jambunathan, S., & Counselman, K. (2002). Parenting attitudes of Asian Indian mothers living in the United States and in India. *Early Child Development & Care, 172*(6), 657–662. https://doi: 10.1080/ 03004430215102

Jamuar, K. (1962). *Study habits of college students.* (*p.* 3-13). Allahabad, India: Indian International Publications.

Jensen, L. A., & Gozkan, A. (2015). Adolescent-parent relations in Asian Indian and Salvadoran immigrant families: a cultural-developmental analysis of autonomy, authority, conflict, and cohesion. *Journal of Research on Adolescence, 25*(2), 340–351. https://doi: 10.1111/jora.12116

Jaser, S.S., Langrock, A.M., Keller, G., Merchant, M.J., Benson, M.A., Reeslund, K.L., Champion, J.E., & Compas, B.E. (2005). Coping with the stress of parental depression II: Adolescent and parent reports of coping and adjustment. *Journal of Clinical Child and*

Adolescent Psychology, 34(1), 193-205. https://doi:10.1207/s15374424jccp3401_18

Jauregui, L. I., Bolanos, R. P., & Garrido, C. O. (2011). Parenting styles and eating disorders. *Journal of Psychiatric and Mental Health Nursing, 18*(8), 728–735. https://doi:10.1111/j.1365-2850.2011. 01723

Jha, J., & Kelleher, F. (2006). *Boys' underachievement in education*. Vancouver, Canada: Ultratech printing limited.

John, Bulus, & Tangsom. (2020). Study Habits and Academic Achievement: A Case Study of Secondary School Science Students in the Jalingo Metropolis, Taraba State, Nigeria. *American Journal of Educational Research, 8*(5), 282-285. https://doi:10.12691/education-8-5-9

John, M. (2010). Students Study Habits and Styles. Retrieved from www.worldwidelearn.com.

Joshi, D., & Dutta, I. (2015). A correlative study of mother parenting style and emotional intelligence of adolescent learner. *International Journal of Innovation and Scientific Research, 13*(1), 145-151.

Kaplan, A., & Maehr, M. L. (2007). The contributions and prospects of goal orientation theory. *Educational Psychology Review 19*(2), 141–184. https://doi:10.1007/s10648-006-9012-5.

Karavasilis, L., Doyle, A., & Markiewicz, D. (2003). Associations between parenting style and attachment to mother in middle childhood and adolescence. *International Journal of Behavioral Development, 27*(2), 153–164.

Katelyn, F. (2013). College Study Habits News. Retrieved from www.studymode.com/essays.

Katerina, A., Alexopoulos, D.A., & Katerina, M. K. (2012). Perceptions of father parenting style, empathy, and self-esteem among Greek preadolescents. *Marriage Family Review, 48*(3), 293–309. https://doi:10.1080/01494929.2012.665016

Katz, L.F. & Windecker-Nelson, B. (2004). Parental meta-emotion philosophy in families with conduct-problem children: Links with peer relations. *Journal of Abnormal Child Psychology, 32*(4), 385-398.

Kaufmann, D., Gesten, E., Santa Lucia, R. C., Salcedo, O., Rendina-Gobioff, G., & Gadd, R. (2000). The relationship between parenting style and children's adjustment: The parents' perspective. *Journal of Child and family studies, 9*(2), 231-245.

Keller, H., & Otto, H. (2009). The cultural socialization of emotion regulation during infancy. *Journal of Cross Cultural Psychology, 40*(6), 996–1011. https://doi:10.1177/0022022109348576

Kelli, K. (2009). Developing Good Study Habits. Retrieved from monster.com. Media/ads. 11/3/2016.

Kelly, W.A. (1998). *Educational Psychology*. Milwaukee, United States: Bruce Publishing Company.

Kenney, Lac, Hummer, Grimaldi, & Labrie. (2014). Pathways of Parenting Style on Adolescents' College Adjustment, Academic Achievement, and Alcohol Risk. *Journal of College Student Retention Research Theory and Practice*, 17(2), 1-14. https://doi: 10.1177/1521025115578232.

Kennedy, P. W., Sheckley, B. G., & Kehrhahn, M. T. (2000). The dynamic nature of student persistence: influence of interactions between student attachment, academic adaptation, and social adaptation [Paper presentation]. In the Annual Meeting of the Association for International Research, Cincinnati.

Keshavarz, S., & Baharudin, R. (2009). Parenting style in a collectivist culture of Malaysia. *European Journal of Social Sciences, 10*(1), 66-73.

Khan, Z. N. (2016). Factors affecting study habits. *World Journal of Educational Research, 3*(1), 145–150. https://doi:10.22158/wjer.v3n1p145

Khurshid, F., Tanveer, A., & Qasmi, F. N. (2012). Relationship between study habits and academic achievement among hostel living and day scholars' university students. *British Journal of Humanities and Social Sciences, 3*(2).

Kliewer, W., Fearnow, M.D., & Miller, P.A. (1996). Coping socialization in middle childhood: Tests of maternal and paternal influences. *Child Development, 67*(5), 2339-2357.

Kliewer. W., Sandler, I., & Wolchik, S. (1994). Family socialization of threat appraisal and coping: Coaching, modeling, and family context. In F. Nestmann & K.Hurrelmann (Eds.), *Social networks and social support in childhood and adolescence. Prevention and intervention in childhood and adolescence* (p. 271-291). Oxford, England: Walter De Gruyter.

Kim, K., & Rohner, R. P. (2002). Parental warmth, control, and involvement in schooling: predicting academic achievement among Korean American adolescents. *Journal of Cross-Cultural Psychology*, 33, 127–140. https://doi:10.1177/0022022102033002001

King, K. A., Vidourek, R. A., & Merianos, A. L. (2016). Authoritarian parenting and youth depression: Results from a national study. *Journal of Prevention & Intervention in the Community, 44*(2), 130–139. https://doi:10.1080/10852352.2016.1132870

Kopko, K. (2007). Parenting styles and adolescents. Cornell Cooperative Extension, Research submitted to Cornell university. Retrieved from http://www.human.cornell.edu/pam/outreach/parenting/research/ upload/Parenting -20Styles-20and-20Adolescents.pdf

Kosterelioglu, I. (2018). Effects of Parenting Style on Students' Achievement Goal Orientation: A Study on High School Students. *Educational Policy Analysis and Strategic Research, 13*(4), 91-107. https://doi: 10.29329/epasr.2018.178.5

Krause, K-L., Bochner, S., & Duchesne, S. (2006). *Educational psychology for learning and teaching*. (2nd. Ed.) South Melbourne, VIC: Thomson Learning Australia.

Kriegbaum, K., Villarreal, B., Wu, V. C., & Heckhausen, J. (2016). Parents still matter: Patterns of shared agency with parents predict college students' academic motivation and achievement. *Motivation Science, 2*(2), 97-115. https://doi.org/10.1037/mot0000033

Kuh, G. D., Kinzie, J., Buckley, J. A., Bridge, B. K., & Hayek, J. C. (2006). What matters to student success: a review of the literature. Commissioned report for the National Symposium on postsecondary student success: spearheading a dialog on student success. Washington, DC: National Postsecondary Education Cooperative.

Kumar, S. (2014). Effect of Parenting Styles on Academic Achievement and Adjustment Problem of Teenage. *International Journal of Engineering, Business and Enterprise Applications, 7*(1), 120-129.

Kuppens, S., Laurent, L., Heyvaert, M., & Onghena, P. (2013). Associations between parental psychological control and relational aggression in children and adolescents: A multilevel and sequential meta-analysis. *Developmental Psychology, 49*(9), 1697–1712. https://doi: 10.1037/a0030740.

Kuppens, S., & Ceulemans, E. (2019). Parenting Styles: A Closer Look at a Well-Known Concept. *Journal of Child and Family Studies, 28*(1), 168–181. https://doi.org/10.1007/s10826-018-1242-x

Lackner, J. M., Gudleski, G. D., & Blanchard, E. B. (2004). Beyond abuse: The association among parenting style, abdominal pain, and somatization in IBS patients. *Behaviour Research and Therapy, 42*(1), 41–56. https://doi:10.1016/S00057967 (03)00069-X

La Torre-Cruz, D., García-Linares, M. C., & Casanova-Arias, P. F. (2014). Relationship between parenting styles and aggressiveness in adolescents. *Electronic Journal of Research in Educational Psychology, 12*(1), 147–169. https://doi.org/10.14204/ejrep.32.13118

Lamborn, S., Mounts, N., Steinberg, L., & Dornbusch, S. M. (1991). Patterns of competence and adjustment from authoritative, authoritarian, indulgent, and neglectful families. *Child Development, 62*(5), 1049-1065. https://doi: 10.2307/1131151

Langrock, A. M., Compas, B. E., Keller, G., Merchant, M. J., & Copeland, M. E. (2002).Coping with the stress of parental depression: Parents' reports of children's coping, emotional, and behavioral problems. *Journal of Clinical Child and Adolescent Psychology, 31*(3), 312-324. https://doi:10.1207/S15374424JCCP3103_03

Lansford, J. E., Godwin, J., Bornstein, M. H., Chang, L., Deater-Deckard, K., Di Giunta, L.,...Skinner, A. T. (2018). Parenting, culture, and the development of externalizing behaviors from age 7 to 14 in nine countries. *Development and Psychopathology, 30*(5), 1937–1958. https://doi:10.1017/S0954579418000925

Lazarus, R.S., & Folkman, S. (1984). *Stress, appraisal, and coping.* New York: Springer.

Lazarus, R. S. (1991). *Emotion and adaptation*. Oxford, NY: Oxford University Press.

Lee, J. K. & Lee, W. K. (2008). The relationship of e-Learner's self-regulatory efficacy and perception of e-Learning environmental quality. *Computers in Human Behavior, 24*(1), 32-47. https://doi:10.1016/j.chb.2006.12.001

Lerdpornkulrat, T., Koul, R., & Sujivorakul, C. (2012). Influence of perceived parenting styles on goal orientations and career aspirations of high school science students in Thailand [Paper presentation]. *In Behavioral Science and Social Problems-010.* 4th International Conference on Humanities and Social Sciences. Faculty of Liberal Arts, Prince of Songkla University, Thailand.

Leung, J., & Shek, D. (2018). Validation of the Perceived Chinese Over parenting Scale in Emerging Adults in Hong Kong. *Journal of Child and Family Studies, 27*(1), 103-117. https://doi:10.1007/s10826-017-0880-8.

Leung, K., Lau, S., & Lam, W. (1998). Parenting Styles and Academic Achievement: A Cross-Cultural Study. *Merrill-Palmer Quarterly, 44*(2), 157-172. Retrieved from http://www.jstor.org/stable/23093664

Ley, K., & Young, D. B. (1998). Self-regulation behaviors in underprepared (developmental) and regular admission college students. *Contemporary Educational Psychology, 23*(1), 42–64. https://doi: 10.1006/ceps.1997.0956

Lieb, R., Wittchen, H. U., Höfler, M., Fuetsch, M., Stein, M. B., & Merikangas, K. R. (2000). Parental psychopathology, parenting styles, and the risk of social phobia in offspring: A prospective-longitudinal community study. *Archives of General Psychiatry, 57*(9), 859–866. https://doi:10.1001/archpsyc.57.9.859

Lin, C. Y. C., & Fu, V. R. (1990). A comparison of child-rearing practices among Chinese, immigrant Chinese, and Caucasian-American parents. *Child Development, 61*(2), 429–433. https://doi: 10.1111/j.1467-8624.1990.tb02789.x

Lin, T. E., & Lian, T. C. (2011). Relationship between Perceived Parenting Styles and Coping Capability among Malaysian Secondary School Students [Paper presentation]. *Proceedings of International Conference on Social Sciences in Singapore*. Retrieved from http://www.ipedr.com/vol5/no1/5-H00032.pdf

Lirias, K., Maarten, P., De Fraine, S., Van Damme, B., & Jan, J. D. (2009). Development of the relation between achievement and academic self-concept in secondary school [Paper presentation]. *American Educational Research Association*. San Diego, CA.

Llorca, A., Richaud, C. M., & Malonda, E. (2017). Parenting, peer relationships, academic selfefficacy, and academic achievement: Direct and mediating effects. *Frontiers in Psychology*, 8, 1664-1078. https://doi:10.3389/fpsyg.2017.02120

Locke, N .M. (1940). The Student Skills Inventory: A study habits test. *Journal of Applied Psychology, 24*(4), 493-504. https://doi.org/10.1037/h0058668

Lola, B., & Shrinidhi, I. (2008). Parenting styles: the impact on student achievement. Marriage & Family Review, 43(1), 14–38. https://doi:10.1080/01494920802010140

Love, & Thomas. (2014). Parenting Styles and Adjustment Outcomes among College Students. *Journal of College Student Development, 55*(2), 139-150. https://doi: 10.1353/csd.2014.0013.

Lowe, H., & Cook, A. (2003). Mind the gap: are students prepared for higher education? *Journal of Further and Higher Education, 27*(1), 53–76. https://doi:10.1080/03098770305629

Luyckx, K., Tildesley, E. A., Soenens, B., Andrews, J. A., Hampson, S. E., Peterson, M., & Duriez, B. (2011). Parenting and trajectories of children's maladaptive behaviors: A 12-year prospective community study. *Journal of Clinical Child &*

Adolescent Psychology, 40(3), 468–478. https://doi:10.1080/15374416. 2011.563470

Lynch, D. J. (2006). Motivational factors, learning strategies and resource management as predictors of course grades. College Student Journal, 40(2), 423–428.

Maccoby, E.E. (1992). The role of parents in the socialization of children: An historical overview. *Developmental Psychology, 28*(6), 1006-1017. https://doi.org/10.1037/0012-1649.28.6.1006

Maccoby, E.E., & Martin, J.A. (1983). Socialization in the context of the family: Parent child interaction. In P.H. Mussen (Series Ed.) & E.M. Hetherington (Vol. Ed.), *Handbook of child psychology*: Socialization, personality, and social development, 4(4), (p. 1-101). New York: Wiley.

Mace, C.A. (2002). The Psychology of Study. Harmondsworth, Middlesex, USA: University of Penguin Book Ltd. Retrieved from http://www.archive.org/details/psychologyofstudOOmace

Maehr, Martin L., & Braskamp, L. A. (1986). *The Motivation Factor: A Theory of Personal Investment*. Lexington, Massachusetts: Lexington Books, 283.

Maehr, M.L., & Meyer, H.A. (1997) .Understanding motivation and schooling: Where we've been, where we are, and where we need to go. *Educational Psychology Review, 9*(4), 371-403. https://www.jstor.org/stable/23359409

Maehr, M. L. (2008). Culture and achievement motivation, *International Journal of Psychology, 43*(5), 917-918. https://doi.org/10.1080/00207590701838162

Mahasneh, A. M. (2014). Investigation the relationship between goal orientation and parenting styles among sample of Jordanian university students. *Educational Research and Reviews, 9*(11), 320-325. https://doi:10.5897/ERR2014.1789.

Mahyuddin, R., Elias, H., & Noordin, N. (2009). Emotional Intelligence, Achievement Motivation and Academic Achievement among Students of the Public and Private Higher Institutions. *The International Journal of Diversity in Organizations, Communities, and Nations, 9*(4), 135-144. https://doi:10.18848/1447-9532/CGP/v09i04/39742.

Mandel, H. P., & Marcus, S. I. (1988). The psychology of under achievement: Differential diagnosis and differential treatment. In I. B. Wiley (Series Ed.), *Wiley series on personality processes*. New York: John Wiley & Sons.

Mannarini, S., Balottin, L., Palmieri, A., & Carotenuto, F. (2018). Emotion regulation and parental bonding in families of adolescents with internalizing and externalizing symptoms. *Frontiers in Psychology*, 9, 1664-1078. https://doi:10.3389/fpsyg.2018.01493.

Markland, D., Ryan, R., Tobin, V., & Rollnick, S. (2005). Motivational Interviewing and Self? Determination Theory. *Journal of Social and Clinical Psychology, 24*(6), 811-831. https://doi:10.1521/jscp.2005.24.6.811.

Marsh, H. W., & Ayotte, V. (2003). Do multiple dimensions of self-concept become more differentiated with age? The differential distinctiveness hypothesis. *Journal of Educational Psychology, 95*(4), 687-706. https://doi.org/10.1037/0022-0663.95.4.687

Martin, W. E., Swartz-Kulstad, J. L., & Madson, M. (1999). Psychosocial factors that predict the college adjustment of first-year undergraduate students: implications for college counselors. Journal of College Counseling, 2(2), 121–133. https://doi.org/10.1002/j.2161-1882.1999.tb00150.x

Martínez, I., Fuentes, M. C., García, F., & Madrid, I. (2013). The parenting style as protective or risk factor for substance use and other behavior problems among Spanish adolescents. Adicciones, 25(3), 235-242. https://doi:10.20882/adicciones.51

Masafoor, S. (2013). The relationship between parenting styles and the educational achievement, *Life Science Journal, 10*(6s), 487-494. http://www.lifesciencesite.com

Maslow, A. (1970). *Motivation and personality*. New York: Harper and Row.

Masud, S. S., Mufarrih, S, H., Qureshi, N, Q., Khan, F., Khan, S., & Khan, M, N. (2019). Academic Performance in Adolescent Students: The Role of Parenting Styles and Socio-Demographic Factors – A Cross Sectional Study from Peshawar, Pakistan,

Frontiers in Psychology, 10, 2497.
https://doi:10.3389/fpsyg.2019.02497

Masud, H., Thurasamy, R., & Ahmad, M. (2014). Parenting styles and academic achievement of young adolescents: A systematic literature review. *Quality and Quantity, 49*(6), 1-13. https://doi:10.1007/s11135-014-0120-x

Mathur, C. (2002). *Manual for Test of study habits & attitudes*. Agra, India: National Psychological Corporation, 3-10.

McClelland, D.C. (1961). *The achieving society*. Princeton, New Jersey: Van Nostrand.

McClelland, D. (1968). *Achievement motivation training for potential high school dropouts*: Achievement Motivation Development Project Working Paper Number 4. Cambridge, MA: Harvard University, Graduate School of Education.

McClelland, D.C., & Winter, D.G. (1969). *Motivating economic achievement*. New York, United States: Free Press.

McClelland, D. C. (1985). *Human motivation*. Chicago, United States: Scott Foresman.

McDaniel, M. A., Howard, D. C., & Einstein, G. O. (2009). The Read-Recite-Review Study Strategy: Effective and Portable. *Psychological Science*, *20*(4), 516–522. https://doi.org/10.1111/j.1467-9280.2009.02325.x

McGregor, J. (2004). Space, Power and the Classroom, *Forum*, *46*(1), 13-23.

McIntyre, J.G., & Dusek, J.B. (1995). Perceived parental rearing practices and styles of coping. *Journal of Youth and Adolescence, 24*(4), 499-509.

McKee, L., Colletti, C., Rakow, A., Jones, D.J., & Forehand, R. (2008). Parenting and child externalizing behaviors: Are the associations specific or diffuse? *Aggression and Violent Behavior, 13*(3), 201-215.

McKinney, C., & Renk, K. (2011). A multivariate model of parent-adolescent relationship variables in early adolescence. *Child Psychiatry and Human Development*, 42, 442–462. https://doi: 10.1007/s10578-011-0228-3

McKinney, C., & Renk, K. (2008). Differential parenting between mothers and fathers. Implications for late adolescents. *Journal of Family Issues, 29*(6), 806–827.

McKenzie, K., & Schweitzer, R. (2001). Who succeeds at university? Factors predicting academic achievement in first year Australian University students. *Higher Education Research and Development, 20*(1), 21-33. https://doi:10.1080/07924360120043621

McLeod, B.D., Weisz, J.R., & Wood, J.J. (2007). Examining the association between parenting and childhood depression: A meta-analysis. *Clinical Psychology Review, 27*(8), 986-1003. https://doi: 10.1016/j.cpr.2007.03.001.

Mehta, P., & Malhotra, D. (1993), Personality, Ability, Motivation and locus of control as predictors of achievement in college Arts students. *The Mind, 19*(1), 1-11.

Menzel, W. E. (1982). How to study effectively. London, England: University Press

Mendezabal, M. J. N. (2013). Study Habits and Attitudes: The Road to Academic Success. *Open Science Repository Education,* Online (open-access), e70081928. doi:10.7392/Education.70081928

Meteyer, K. B., & Perry-Jenkins, M. (2009). Dyadic parenting and children's externalizing symptoms. *Family Relations: An Interdisciplinary Journal of Applied Family Studies, 58*(3), 289–302. https://doi.org/10.1111/j.1741-3729.2009.00553.x

Middleton, M., & Midgley, C. (1997). Avoiding the demonstration of lack of ability: An underexplored aspect of goal theory. *Journal of Educational Psychology, 89*(4), 710-718. https://doi: 10.1037/0022-0663.89.4.710.

Miller, P.A., Kliewer, W., & Partch, J. (2010). Socialization of children's recall and use of strategies for coping with interparental conflict. *Journal of Child and Family Studies, 19*(4), 429-443. https://doi:10.1007/s10826-009-9314-6

Milevsky, A., Schlechter, M., Netter, S., & Keehn, D. (2007). Maternal and paternal parenting styles in adolescents: Associations with self-esteem, depression and life satisfaction. *Journal of Child and*

Family Studies, 16(1), 39–47. https://doi:10.1007/s10826-006-9066-5

Milevsky, A., Schlechter, M., Klem, L., & Kehl, R. (2008). Constellations of maternal and paternal parenting styles in adolescence: Congruity and well-being. *Marriage & Family Review, 44*(1), 81–98. https://doi:10.1080/01494920802185447

Mishra, K. N. (1992). Adjustment, self-concept, test anxiety and desirable study habits: as predictors of academic achievement. *The Asian Journal Psychology of Education, 25*(7-8), 21-26.

Moffitt, T. E. (1993). Adolescence-limited and life-course-persistent antisocial behavior: A developmental taxonomy. *Psychological Review, 100*(4), 674–701. https://doi.org/10.1037/0033-295X.100.4.674

Mohan, V., Kaur, M., Kaur, B. (2013). Achievement Motivation and Self-Concept of Adolescents: Significance of Parental Attitude. *Indian Journal of Psychological Science, 4*(1), 020-022.

Moitra, T., & Mukherjee, I. (2012). Does parenting behavior impact delinquency? A comparative study of delinquents and non-delinquents. *International Journal of Criminal Justice Sciences, 5*(2), 274-285.

Moos, H. R. (1993). *Manual for coping responses inventory.* United States: Psychological Assessment Resources, Inc., 3-10.

Morris, A.S., Silk J.S., Steinberg, L., Myers, S.S., & Robinson, L.R. (2007). The role of the family context in the development of emotion regulation. *Social Development, 16*(2), 361-388. https://doi:10.1111/j.1467-9507.2007.00389.x

Mousavi, S. E., Low, W. Y., & Hashim, A. H. (2016). Perceived parenting styles and cultural influences in adolescent's anxiety: A cross-cultural comparison. *Journal of Child and Family Studies, 25*(7), 2102– 2110. https://doi:10.1007/s10826-016-0393-x

Muller, C., & Kerbow, D. (1993). Parent involvement in the home, school, and community. In Schneider, B., and Coleman, J. S. (eds.), *Parents, Their Children, and Schools* (p. 13-39). Boulder, Colorado: Westview Press.

Murray, A. (2012). The relationship of parenting style to academic achievement in middle childhood, *The Irish Journal of Psychology, 33*(4), 137-152. https://doi:10.1080/03033910.2012.724645

Murray, H. (1938). *Explorations in personality*. Oxford, NY: Oxford University Press.

Nagaraju, M. T. (2004). *Study Habits of Secondary School Students*. New Delhi, India: Discovery Publishing House

Nancy, D., & Laurance, S. (1993). Parenting style as context: An integrative model. *Psychological Bulletin, 113*(3), 487–496. https://doi:10.1037/0033-2909.113.3.487

Narahari, B. G. & Tewari, A. (2015). The Impact of Academic Counseling on Study Habits of Adolescent Students-in Indian Government Schools. *International Journal of Education and Psychological Research, 4*(1), 1-5.

Nelson, L. J., Walker, L. M., Christensen, K. J., Evans, C. A., & Carroll, J. S. (2011). Parenting in emerging adulthood: an examination of parenting clusters and correlates. *Journal of Youth and Adolescence, 40*(6), 730–743. https://doi: 10.1007/s10964-010-9584-8

Neumeister, K. (2004). Understanding the Relationship between Perfectionism and Achievement Motivation in Gifted College Students. *Gifted Child Quarterly, 48*(3), 219-231. https://doi:10.1177/001698620404800306.

Nikki, K. (2013). Common Bad Study Habits. Retrieved from www.newa4jax.com2/4/2016.

Nimbalkar, A. S., Shukla, V. V., Phatak, A. G., & Nimbalkar, S. M. (2013). Newborn care practices and health seeking behavior in urban slums and villages of Anand, Gujarat. *Indian Paediatrics, 50*(4), 408–410. https://doi:10.1007/s13312-013-0116-y

Noar, S. M., Anderman, E. M., Zimmerman, R. S. & Cupp, P. K. (2005). Fostering Achievement Motivation in Health Education, *Journal of Psychology & Human Sexuality, 16*(4), 59-76.

Nourian, A., Shah, M. F., Mousavi, N. S. N., Nourian, (2011). A. Study skills and habits of the students in Tehran Islamic Azad

University of medical sciences in the academic year 2008–2009. *Strides in Development of Medical Education Journal, 7*(2), 104–111.

Nuthanap, G. (2007). Gender Analysis of Academic Achievement among High School Students, Thesis submitted to the Department of Human Development, College of Rural Home Science, Dharwad University of Agricultural Sciences. Dharwad, India.

Nyarko, K. (2011). The influence of authoritative parenting style on adolescents' academic achievement. *American Journal of Social and Management Sciences, 2*(3), 278-282.

Oğuz, A. (1999). The effect of lecture note taking on the level of learning and recalling. Doctoral Thesis, Hacettepe University Institute of Educational Science, Ankara, Turkey.

Okorodudu, G. N. (2010). Influence of parenting styles on adolescent delinquency in delta central senatorial district. Edo Journal of Counselling, 3(1). https://doi:10.4314/ejc.v3i1.52682.

Oladele, J. O. (2004). Fundamentals of educational psychology. Handbook for Education students and teachers. Lagos, Nigeria: Johns-Lads Publishers Ltd.

Orgilés, M., Penosa, P., Morales, A., Fernández-Martínez, I., & Espada, J. P. (2018). Maternal anxiety and separation anxiety in children aged between 3 and 6 years: The mediating role of parenting style. *Journal of Developmental & Behavioral*

Pediatrics, 39(8), 621–628. https://doi:10.1097/DBP. 0000000000000593

Oxford, R., Park-Oh, Y., Ito, S., & Sumrall, M. (1993). Japanese by satellite: Effects of motivation, language learning styles and strategies, gender, course level, and previous language learning experience on Japanese language achievement. *Foreign Language Annals, 26*(3), 358-371.

Pajares, F. (1996). Self-efficacy in academic settings. *Review of Educational Research, 66*(4), 543-578. https://doi.org/10.3102%2F00346543066004543

Parker, J., & Johnson, C. (1981). Affecting Achievement Motivation. Charlottesville, Virginia: University of Virginia. (ERIC Document Reproduction Service Number ED 226 833)

Pascarella, E., & Terenzini, P. T. (2005). How college affects students. A third decade of research. San Francisco, United States: Jossey-Bass.

Patel, Amin, N., & Power, T. (2002). Modernity and childrearing in families of Gujarati Indian adolescents. *International Journal of Psychology, 37*(4), 239–245.

Patel, B. V. (1976) .*Manual for study habits inventory,* Agra, India: Agra Psychological Research cell, 1-8.

Patel, D. V., Bansal, S. C., Nimbalkar, A. S., Phatak, A. G., Nimbalkar, S. M., & Desai, R. G. (2015). Breastfeeding practices, demographic variables, and their association with morbidities in children. *Advances in Preventive Medicine*, Article ID 892825. https://doi:10.1155/2015/892825

Pathak, S. (2020). Academic stress and self-efficacy in relation to study habits among adolescents. *The International Journal of Indian Psychology, 8*(3), 1735 – 1743. https:/doi: 10.25215/0803.178

Patrick, H., & Ryan, A. (2008). What Do Students Think About When Evaluating Their Classroom's Mastery Goal Structure? An Examination of Young Adolescents' Explanations. *Journal of Experimental Education*, *77*(2), 99-124. https://doi:10.3200/JEXE.77.2.99-124.

Patrick W. L., Leung, & Kim. (1998). Parenting Styles, Motivational Orientations, and Self-Perceived Academic Competence: A Mediatorial Model. *Merrill-Palmer Quarterly, 44*(1), 1-19.

Paulson, S. E. (1994). Relations of parenting style and parental involvement with ninth-Grade students' achievement. *Journal of Early Adolescence, 14*(2), 250-267. https://doi.org/10.1177%2F027243169401400208

Pellerin, L. A. (2005). Applying Baumrind's parenting typology to high schools: Toward a middle-range theory of authoritative socialization. *Social Science Research, 34*(2), 283-303. https://doi.org/10.1016/j.ssresearch.2004.02.003

Perez, J. C., Cumsille, P., & Martinez, M. L. (2016). Brief report: agreement between parent and adolescent autonomy expectations and its relationship to adolescent adjustment. *Journal of Adolescence*, 53, 10–15. https://doi: 10.1016/j.adolescence.2016. 08.010

Petersen, I. H., Louw, J., & Dumont, K. (2009). Adjustment to university and academic performance among disadvantaged students in South Africa. *Educational Psychology: An International Journal of Experimental Educational Psychology, 29*(1), 99–115.

Peterson, G. W., Steinmetz, S. K., & Wilson, S. M. (eds). (2005). *Parent-Youth Relations: Cultural and Cross-Cultural Perspectives*. New York, NY: Hawthorn Press.

Pintrich, P. R. (2004). A conceptual framework for assessing motivation and self-regulated learning in college students. *Educational Psychology Review, 16*(4), 385–407.

Pintrich, P. R. (2000). An achievement goal theory perspective on issues in motivation terminology, theory and research. *Contemporary Educational Psychology, 25*(1), 92-104. https://doi.org/10.1006/ceps.1999.1017

Pong, S., Johnston J., & Chen V. (2010). Authoritarian parenting and Asian adolescent school performance: Insights from the US and Taiwan. *International Journal of Behavior Development, 34*(1), 62-72. http://dx.doi.org/10.1177/0165025409345073

Pong S. L., Lingxin, H., & Erica, G. (2005). The roles of parenting styles and social capital in the school performance of immigrant

Asian and Hispanic adolescents. *Social Science Quarterly, 86*(4), 928–950. https://doi.org/10.1111/j.0038-4941.2005.00364.x

Power, T. G. (2013). Parenting dimensions and styles: A brief history and recommendations for future research. *Childhood Obesity, 9*(s1), S14–S21. https://doi:10.1089/chi.2013.0034

Power T. G. (2013). Parenting dimensions and styles: a brief history and recommendations for future research. *Childhood obesity (Print), 9 Suppl* (Suppl 1), S14–S21. https://doi.org/10.1089/chi.2013.0034

Premalakshmi, K. (2012). Study habits and academic achievement of higher secondary students. *Scholarly Research Journal for Interdisciplinary Studies, 1*(3), 551-565.

Querido, J. G., Warner, T. D., & Eyberg, S. M. (2002). Parenting styles and child behaviour in African American families of preschool children. *Journal of Clinical Child & Adolescent Psychology, 31*(2), 272–277. https://doi:10.1207/S15374424JCCP3102_12

Rahimpour, P., Direkvand-Moghadam, A., Direkvand-Moghadam, A., & Hashemian, A. (2015). Relationship between the parenting styles and students' educational performance among Iranian girl high school students, a cross-sectional study. *Journal of Clinical and Diagnostic Research, 9*(12), JC05–JC07. https://doi:10.7860/JCDR/2015/15981.6914

Rajendran, K., Kruszewski, E., & Halperin, J. M. (2016). Parenting style influences bullying: A longitudinal study comparing children with and without behavioral problems. *Journal of Child Psychology and Psychiatry, 57*(2), 188–195. https://doi:10.1111/jcpp.12433

Ramaswamy, R. (1990). Study habits and Academic Achievement. *Experiment Education, 18*(10), 255- 260.

. Rani, R. (2013). Relationship between Home Environment and Study Habit of Senior Secondary School Students. *International Journal for Research in Education, 2*(7), 38-42.

Reitman, D., Rhode, P., Hupp, S. D. A., & Altobello, C. (2002). Development and validation of the Parental Authority Questionnaire–Revised. *Journal of Psychopathology and Behavioral Assessment, 24*, 119-127. https://doi.org/10.1023/A:1015344909518

Registrar General of India. (2011). Census of India 2011: Provisional population totals-India data sheet. New Delhi, India: Office of the Registrar General & Census Commissioner.

Renk, K., & Smith, T. (2007). Predictors of Academic-Related Stress in College Students: An Examination of Coping, Social Support, Parenting, and Anxiety, *NASPA Journal, 44*(3), 405-431. https://doi:10.2202/1949-6605.1829

Rezaie, L. H., Seyed, F. S. F., Reza, M. S., Chehrzad, M. M., Kazem, N. L. E. (2017). The relationship between the study habits and the academic performance of medical sciences students. *Journal of Holistic Nursing and Midwifery, 27*(2), 65–73. https://doi:10.18869/acadpub.hnmj.27.2.65

Ricard, N., & Pelletier, L. (2016). Dropping out of high school: The role of parent and teacher self-determination support, reciprocal friendships and academic motivation. *Contemporary Educational Psychology*, 44/45, 32-40. https://doi: 10.1016/j.cedpsych.2015.12.003

Rienties, B., Beausaert, S., Grohnert, T., Niemantsverdriet, S., & Kommers, P. (2012). Understanding academic performance of international students: the role of ethnicity, academic and social integration. *Higher Education, 63*(6), 685–700.

Rim, & Scheictewr. (2002). Relation among achievement, self-concept and motivation in mathematics and language arts: A longitudinal study. *Journal of Experimental Education, 67* (2), 135-149.

Rinaldi, C. M., & Howe, N. (2012). Mothers' and fathers' parenting styles and associations with toddlers' externalizing, internalizing, and adaptive behaviors. *Early Childhood Research Quarterly, 27* (2), 266–273. https://doi:10.1016/j.ecresq.2011.08.001

Riveiro, J. M. S., Cabanach, R.G., & Arias, A.V. (2001). Multiple-goal pursuit and its relation to cognitive, self-regulatory and motivational strategies. *British Journal of Educational*

Psychology, 71(4), 561- 572. https://doi.org/10.1348/000709901158677

Riverse, J. R. (2008). *The Relationship Between Parenting Styles and Academic Achievement and The Mediating Influence of Motivation, Goal-Oriented and Academic Self-Efficacy*. Doctoral dissertation: Florida State University, Florida. Retrieved from http://purl.flvc.org/fsu/fd/FSU_migr_etd-1875

Robinson, F. (1990). Principles and Procedures in Student Counselling. New York, United States: Harper and Row.

Robbins, S. B., Lauver, K., Le, H., Davis, D., Langley, R., & Carlstrom, A. (2004). Do psychosocial and study skill factors predict college outcomes? A meta-analysis. *Psychological Bulletin, 130*(2), 261–288. https://doi: 10.1037/0033-2909.130.2.261

Roche, K. M., Ensminger M. E., & Cherlin A. J. (2007). Parenting style and adolescent outcomes among African and Latino families living in low income. *Journal of Family Issue, 11*(23), 882-909. http://dx.doi.org/10.1177/0192513X07299617

Rooij, C. M., Jansen, P. W. A., & Grift, J. C. M. (2018). First-year university students' academic success: the importance of academic adjustment. *European Journal of Psychology of Education. 33*(4), 749–767. https://doi:10.1007/s10212-017-0347-8

Roopnarine, J. L., Talukder, E., Jain, D., Joshi, P., & Srivastav, P. (1990). Characteristics of holding, patterns of play, and social behaviors between parents and infants in New Delhi, India. *Developmental Psychology, 26*(4), 667–673. https://doi:10.1037/0012-1649.26.4.667

Roskam, I., Stievenart, M., Meunier, J. C., & Noël, M. P. (2014). The development of children's inhibition: Does parenting matter? *Journal of Experimental Child Psychology, 122*(1), 166–182. https://doi:10.1016/j.jecp. 2014.01.003

Rossman, B. B. R., & Rea, J. G. (2005). The relation of parenting styles and inconsistencies to adaptive functioning for children in conflictual and violent families. *Journal of Family Violence, 20*(5), 261–277. https://doi: 10.1007/s10896-005-6603-8

Rotter, J. B. (1966). Generalized expectancies for internal versus external control of reinforcement. *Psychological Monographs: General and Applied, 80*(1), 1-28. https://doi.org/10.1037/h0092976

Ruch, F.L. (1995). *Psychology and Life*. New York, United States: Scot Freeman and Co.

Ryan, R. M., & Stiller, J. (1991). The social contexts of internalization: Parent and teacher influences on autonomy, motivation and learning. In P.R. Pintrich & M. L. Maehr (Eds.). *Advances in Motivation and achievement*, (p. 115-149), Greenwich, CT: Jai Press.

Sarangi, C. (2015). Achievement motivation of the high school students: a case study among different communities of Goalpara district of Assam. *Journal of Education and Practice, 6*(19), 140-144.

Saraswathi, T. S., & Ganapathy, H. (2002). Indian parents' ethno theories as reflections of the Hindu scheme of child and human development. In H. Keller, & Y. H. Poortinga (Eds.), *Between culture and biology: Perspectives on ontogenetic development* (p. 79-88). New York, US: Cambridge University Press. http://dx.doi.org/10.1017/CBO9780511489853.005

Sarwar, S. (2016). Influence of Parenting Style on Children's Behaviour. *Journal of Education and Educational Development, 3*(2), 222-244.

Sawar, M., Bashir, M., Khan, N. M., & Kahn, S. M. (2009). Study-orientation of High and Low Academic achievers at Secondary level in Pakistan. *Educational Research and Reviews, 4*(4), 204-207. https://www.academicjournals.org/ERR, April.

Schunk, D. H. (1996). Self-efficacy for learning and performance, The Annual Conference of the American Educational Research Association, New York, NY. Retrieved from http://files.eric.ed.gov/fulltext/ED394663.pdf

Seema, K. N., & Begum, K. (2008). Childrearing practices among Kurubas and Soliga tribes from South India. *Studies of Tribes and Tribals, 6*(1), 59–62. https://doi:10.1080/0972639X.2008.11886576

Senecal, C., Koestner, R., & Vallerand, R. (1995). Self-regulation and academic procrastination. *The Journal of Social Psychology, 135*(5), 607-619.

Sevinç, S., & Gizir, C. A. (2014). Factors negatively affecting university adjustment from the views of first-year university students: the case of Mersin University. Educational Sciences: Theory & Practice, 14(4), 1301– 1308.

Sharma, E. (2009). Relationship of creativity with academic achievement, achievement motivation, self-concept and levels of adjustment among adolescents. Doctoral thesis, Institute of Advance Studies in Education, Faculty of Education, Jamia Millia Islamia University.

Shaw, D. S., Keenan, K., & Vondra, J. I. (1994). Developmental precursors of externalizing behavior: ages 1 to 3. *Developmental Psychology; 30*(3), 355–364. https://doi: 10.1037/0012-1649.30.3.355.

Shaw, J G. *(1955)*. An evaluation of study skills course*. Personnel and Guidance Journal*, 33, 465-468.

Shek, D. T. L. (2002). Family functioning and psychological well-being, school adjustment, and problem behavior in Chinese adolescents with and without economic disadvantage. *The Journal of Genetic Psychology: Research and Theory on Human*

Development, 163(4), 497-502. https://doi.org/10.1080/00221320209598698

Shelke, M. (2019). Effective study habits for learners [Paper presentation]. National Seminar on Emerging Innovative Teaching and Leaning Strategies in Nursing Education, 38-40.

SheRa. (2012). Study Habit and its impact on secondary school students. Doctoral thesis, Jamia Millia Islamia University, New delhi.

Shih, S. (2005). Role of achievement goals in children's learning in Taiwan. *Journal of Educational Research, 98*(5), 310-320.

Shipman, K.L., & Zeman, J. (2001). Socialization of children's emotion regulation in mother-child dyads: A developmental psychopathology perspective. *Development and Psychopathology*, 13(2), 317-336. https://doi.org/10.1017/S0954579401002073

Siahi, E. A, & Maiyo, J. K. (2015). Study of the relationship between study habits and academic achievement of students: A case of Spicer Higher Secondary School, India. *International Journal of Educational Administration and Policy Studies, 7*(7), 134-141. https://doi: 10.5897/IJEAPS2015.0404

Siddiqui, M. A., & Fatima, T. (2014). Study of academic achievement in relation to study habits and achievement motivation among Muslim and non-Muslim adolescents. *Indian Journal of Research, 3*(4), 66-69. http://www.worldwidejournals.com/paripex/

Sikhwari, T. D. (2014). A study of the Relationship between Motivation Self Concept and Academic Achievement of Students at a University of Limpopo Province, South Africa. *International Journal of Educational Science, 6*(1), 19-25.

Silk, J.S., Shaw, D.S., Skuban, E.M., Oland, A.A. & Kovacs, M. (2006). Emotion regulation strategies in offspring of childhood-onset depressed mothers. *Journal of Child Psychology and Psychiatry, 47*(1), 69-78.

Simons, L. G., & Conger, R. D. (2007). Linking mother–father differences in parenting to a typology of family parenting styles and adolescent outcomes. *Journal of Family Issues, 28*(2), 212–241. https://doi:10.1177/0192513X06294593

Skinner, E.A., Edge, K., Altman, J., & Sherwood, H. (2003). Searching for the structure of coping: A review and critique of category systems for classifying ways of coping. *Psychological Bulletin, 129*(2), 216-269.

Smetana, J. G. (1995). Parenting styles and conceptions of parental authority during adolescence. *Child Development, 66*(2), 299–316. https://doi: 10.2307/1131579.

Smith, C.L. (2006). Children's coping strategies and coping efficacy: Relations to parent socialization, child adjustment, and familial alcoholism. *Development and Psychopathology, 18*(2), 445-469. https://doi: 10.1017/S095457940606024X.

Snell, W., Overbey, G., & Brewer, L. (2005). Parenting Perfectionism and the Parenting Role. *Personality and Individual Differences, 39*(3), 613-624. https://doi:10.1016/j.paid.2005.02.006.

Solomon, R.H. (1999). Personal Adjustment to Reading Success and Failure, Clinical Studies in Reading. London, England: McGraw-Hill.

Sorkhabi, N., & Middaugh, E. (2013). How Variations in Parents' Use of Confrontive and Coercive Control Relate to Variations in Parent–Adolescent Conflict, Adolescent Disclosure, and Parental Knowledge: Adolescents' Perspective. *Journal of Child and Family Studies, 23*(7), 1227–1241. https://doi:10.1007/s10826-013-9783-5.

Sorkhabi, N. (2005). Applicability of Baumrind's parent typology to collective cultures: Analysis of cultural explanations of parent socialization effects. *International Journal of Behavioral Development, 29*(6), 552–563. https://doi:10.1177/01650250500172640

Spinath, B., Spinath, F. M., Harlaar, N., & Plomin, R. (2006). Predicting school achievement from general cognitive ability, self-perceived ability, and intrinsic value. *Intelligence*, 34, 363–374. https://doi:10.1016/j.intell.2005.11.004

Steele, E. H., & McKinney, C. (2018). Emerging adult psychological problems and parenting style: Moderation by parent-child relationship quality. Personality and Individual Differences, 146, 201-208. https://doi:10.1016/ j.paid.2018.04.048

Steinberg, L., & Silk, J. S. (2002). Parenting adolescents. In M. H. Bornstein (Ed.), *Handbook of parenting: Children and parenting* (p. 103–133). New Jersey, United States: Lawrence Erlbaum Associates Publishers.

Steinberg, L., Lamborn, S., Darling, N., Mounts, N., & Dornbusch, S. (1994). Over-time changes in adjustment and competence among adolescents from authoritative, authoritarian, indulgent, and neglectful families. *Child Development*, 65(3), 754-770. https://doi.org/10.2307/1131416

Stocker, C.M., Richmond, M.K., & Rhoades, G.K. (2007). Family emotional processes and adolescents' adjustment. *Social Development, 16*(2), 310 325.

Stormshak, E. A., Bierman, K. L., McMahon, R. J., & Lengua, L. J. (2000). Parenting practices and child disruptive behavior problems in early elementary school. *Journal of Clinical Child Psychology, 29*(1), 17–29. https://doi:10.1207/S15374424jccp2901_3

Strage, A., & Brandt, T. S. (1999). Authoritative parenting and college students' academic adjustment and success. *Journal of Educational Psychology, 91*(1), 146-456.

Strage. (1998). Family context variables and the development of self-regulation in college students. Adolescence, 33(129), 17-31.

Stumm Von, S., Hell, B., Chamorro-Premuzic, T. (2011). The Hungry Mind: Intellectual Curiosity Is the Third Pillar of Academic Performance. *Perspective on Psychological Science, 6*(6), 574–588.

Suet-ling, P., Jamie, J., & Vivien, C. (2010). Authoritarian parenting and Asian adolescent school performance: insights from the US and Taiwan. *International Journal of Behavioral Development, 34*(1), 62–72. https://doi:10.1177/0165025409345073

Tam, C. L., Chong, S. M., Kadirvelu, A., & Khoo, Y. T. (2012). Parenting Styles and Self-Efficacy of Adolescents: Malaysian Scenario. *Global Journal of Human Social Science Research, 12*(14 (Version 1)), 19-25.

Tamsen, C., & Livingston, J. (1999). The differential impact of motivation on the self-regulated strategy use of high- and low-achieving college students. *Journal of College Student Development, 40*(1), 54-60.

Tanaka, & Yamauchi. (2000). Causal models of achievement motive, goal orientation, intrinsic interest, and academic achievement in classroom. *Shinrigaku kenkyu: The Japanese journal of psychology, 71*(4), 317-324. https://doi:10.4992/jjpsy.71.317.

Tang, J., Li, N., Sandoval, J., & Liu, Y. (2018). Parenting Styles and Academic Motivation: A Sample from Chinese High Schools. *Journal of Child and Family Studies, 27*(10), 3395-3401. https://doi:10.1007/s10826-018-1164-7.

Tella, A. (2007). The impact of motivation on student's academic achievement and learning outcomes in mathematics among secondary school students in Nigeria. *Eurasia Journal of Mathematics, Science & Technology Education,* 3(2), 149-156. https://doi.org/10.12973/ejmste/75390

Thakre, N., & Gupte, M. (2016). Effect of perceived parenting styles on Aggression and Emotional intelligence among adolescents. *International Journal of Informative & Futuristic Research, 4*(1), 4892-4900. http://ijifr.com/searchjournal.aspx

Thergaonkar, N. R., & Wadkar, A. J. (2007). Relationship between test anxiety and parenting style. *Journal of Indian Association for Child and Adolescent Mental Health, 3*(1), 10–12. https://eric.ed.gov/?id=EJ896856

Thompson, R.A., & Meyer, S. (2007). The socialization of emotion regulation in the family. In J. Gross (Ed.), *Handbook of emotion regulation* (p. 249-268). New York, United States: Guilford.

Trinkner, R., Cohn, E. S., Rebellon, C. J., & Van Gundy, K. (2012). Don't trust anyone over 30: parental legitimacy as a mediator between parenting style and changes in delinquent behavior over time. *Journal of Adolescence, 35*(1), 119–132. https://doi:10.1016/j.adolescence.2011.05.003

Tucker, C. M., Zayco, R. A., & Herman, K. C. (2002). Teacher and child variables as predictors of academic engagement among low-income African American children. *Psychology in the Schools, 39*(4), 477 - 488.

Turner, E. A., Chandler, M., & Heffer, R. W. (2009). The influence of parenting styles, achievement motivation, and self-efficacy on academic performance in college students. *Journal of College Student Development, 50*(3), 337–346. https://doi:10.1353/csd.0.0073

Turner, L. A., & Johnson, B. (2003). A model of mastery motivation for at-risk pre-schoolers. *Journal of Educational Psychology, 95*(3), 495-505.

Tuzgöl, M. (1998). Examining aggressiveness levels of high school students whose parents have different attitudes in terms of various variable. Doctoral Thesis, Hacettepe University, Ankara, Turkey.

Vijayalakshmi. (1995). Relationship of Father's economic condition with intelligence and ability of school students. *Asian Journal of Psychology and Education, 28*(7-8), 1-5.

Wang, W., & Leichtman, M. D. (2000). Same beginnings, different stories: A comparison of American and Chinese children's narratives. *Child Development, 71*(5), 1329-1346. https://doi:10.1111/1467-8624.00231

Want, J., & Kleitman, S. (2006). Imposter phenomenon and self-handicapping: Links with parenting styles and self-confidence.

Personality and Individual Differences, 40(5), 961-971. https://doi:10.1016/j. paid.2005.10.005

Williams, L. R., Degnan, K. A., Perez-Edgar, K. E., Henderson, H. A., Rubin, K. H., Pine, D. S.,...Fox, N. A. (2009). Impact of behavioral inhibition and parenting style on internalizing and externalizing problems from early childhood through adolescence. *Journal of Abnormal Child Psychology, 37*(8), 1063-1075. https://doi:10.1007/s10802-009-9331-3

Williams, K. E., Ciarrochi, J., & Heaven, P. C. (2012). Inflexible parents, inflexible kids: A 6-year longitudinal study of parenting style and the development of psychological flexibility in adolescents. *Journal of Youth and Adolescence, 41*(8), 1053-1066. https://doi:10.1007/s10964-012-9744-0

Willcoxson, L., Cotter, J., & Joy, S. (2011). Beyond the first-year experience: the impact on attrition of student experiences throughout undergraduate degree studies in six diverse universities. *Studies in Higher Education, 36*(3), 331-352.

Wintre, M. G., Dilouya, B., Pancer, S. M., Pratt, M. W., Birnie-Lefcovitch, S., Polivy, J., & Adams, G. (2011). *Higher Education, 62*(4), 467–481.

Wischerth, Mulvaney, Brackett, Perkins, & Donna. (2016). The Adverse Influence of Permissive Parenting on Personal Growth and the Mediating Role of Emotional Intelligence. *The Journal of*

Genetic Psychology, 177(5). 185-189. https://doi:10.1080/00221325.2016.1224223.

Wittenborn, J. R., Larsen, R. P., & Mogils, R. L. (1945). An empirical evaluation of study habits for college courses in French and Spanish. *Journal of Educational Psycholo*gy, *36*(8), 449-474. https://doi.org/10.1037/h0054441

Wolff, K. S. (2001). Rewards for Middle School Student, Thesis submitted to Faculty of Pacific Lutheran University, United States, UMI Number: 1406569.

Wolfradt, U., Hempel, S., & Miles, J. N. (2003). Perceived parenting styles, depersonalisation, anxiety and coping behaviour in adolescents. *Personality and Individual Differences, 34*(3), 521-532. https://doi:10.1016/S0191-8869(02)00092-2

Woollfolk, A. (2004). *Educational psychology*. Boston, Massachusetts: Allyn & Bacon.

Wrenn, C. G. (1934). *Study-habits inventory.* Palo Alto, California: Stanford University Press.

Wrenn, C. G., Humber. (1941). *Manual of the directions of the study habit inventory*, *Revised edition*, Palo Alto, California: Stanford University Press.

Xitao, F., & Michael, C. (2001). Parental Involvement and Students' Academic Achievement: A Meta-Analysis. *Educational Psychology Review, 13*(1), 1-22.

Yahaya, A., & Nordin, K. (2006). Relationship between Self Concepts, Motivation, and Parenting Styles Effected Students Achievements. Research project submitted to Faculty of Education: Universiti Technology Malaysia.

Yao, S. (2010). Coping and involuntary responses to stress in Chinese university students: Psychometric properties of the responses to stress questionnaire. *Journal of Personality Assessment, 92*(4), 356-361.

Yasmin, S., Kiani, A., & Chaudry, A. G. (2014). Parenting styles as a predictors of academic achievement of students. *International Journal of Technical Research and Applications, 2*(6), 28-31. http://muse.jhu.edu/journals/csd/summary/v050/50-3.turner.html

Yazdani, K., & Godbole, V. (2014). Studying the role of habits and achievement motivation in improving students' academic performance. *European Online Journal of Natural and Social Sciences, 3*(4), 827-839.

Zaborskis, A., Sirvyte, D., & Zemaitiene, N. (2016). Prevalence and familial predictors of suicidal behaviour among adolescents in Lithuania: A cross-sectional survey 2014. *BMC Public Health,* 16, 554. https://doi:10.1186/s12889-016-3211-x

Zhang, W. X., & Fuligni, A. J. (2006). Authority, autonomy, and family relationships among adolescents in urban and rural China.

Journal of Research on Adolescence, 16(4), 527-537. https://doi: 10.1111/j.1532-7795.2006.00506.x

Zhang, W. X., Wang, M. P., & Fuligni, A. J. (2006). Expectations for autonomy, beliefs about parental authority, and parent-adolescent conflict and cohesion. *Acta Psychologica Sinica, 38*(6), 868–876.

Zhang, W., Wei, X., Ji, L., Chen, L., & Deater-Deckard, K. (2017). Reconsidering parenting in Chinese culture: subtypes, stability, and change of maternal parenting style during early adolescence. *Journal of Youth and Adolescence, 46*(5), 1117-1136. https://doi: 10.1007/s10964-017-0664-x

Zimmer-Gembeck, M. J., & Locke, E. M. (2007). The socialization of adolescent coping behaviors: Relationships with families and teachers. *Journal of Adolescence, 30*(1), 1-16. https://doi:10.1016/j.adolescence.2005.03.001

Zong, X., Zhang, L., & Yao, M. (2018). Parental involvement and Chinese elementary students' achievement goals: the moderating role of parenting style. *Educational Studies, 44*(3), 341-356. https://doi:10.1080/03055698.2017.1373634

Zupancic, M., Podlesek, A., & Kavcic, T. (2004). Parental child care practices of Slovenian pre-schoolers mothers and fathers: The family environment questionnaire. *Horizons of Psychology, 13*(3), 7-26.

Zurcher, J. D., Holmgren, H. G., Coyne, S. M., Barlett, C. P., & Yang, C. (2018). Parenting and cyberbullying across adolescence. *Cyber psychology, Behavior, and Social Networking, 21*(5), 294-303. https://doi:10. 1089/cyber.2017.0586

CPSIA information can be obtained
at www.ICGtesting.com
Printed in the USA
LVHW040105060123
736479LV00011B/872

9 784733 62815